_____

Name

_____

Start Date

_____

Finish Date

GAIL OKULEY

HIS
HANDS
MY FEET

Journey through the
miracles of Jesus

STUDY
JOURNAL

DEDICATION

To my amazing and adventuresome husband Gordon,
who lovingly and persistently encouraged me to complete this work;
who willingly stretched alongside me in these unexpected revelations;
and who landed my first consultation with the publisher!

ACKNOWLEDGMENTS

The Lord is full of blessings and surprises that will change the trajectory of our lives. I could not have been more unsuspecting, as I began taking notes during a sermon by my pastor, Kent Yorgey. He poised two gripping questions that ultimately sparked this entire book!

Another special blessing has been a *Jonathan and David relationship,* with my friend Sharon Mullay, who has heard most of this *first* and has faithfully encouraged me to keep sharing these deep revelations.

Eric Bugbee, Blue Trail Productions, insisted that my *Along the Way* stories be in *every* chapter, not just the twelve I had originally planned to do.

Dr. Caroline Oda, (Oahu, Hawaii), surprised me one day when she graciously offered to edit this entire manuscript, much to my delight.

My sister, Marsha Cook also came alongside me eagerly, for discussion and further editing.

Publisher Michael Stickler graciously opened the door for my first consult unexpectedly at the National Religious Broadcasters conference in 2023 and readily accepted my manuscript within a few weeks! I appreciate his wise recommendation to "take the bridle off the horse" and expand my Along the Way stories.

He assigned me to work with Naomi Ruth Inman, Executive Editor, who has amazed me with her wonderful expertise, encouragement, and friendship!

Dr. Ed Silvoso and Dave Thompson, Transform Our World, radically transformed our mindsets since we first met in 2011, to accept our responsibility for the Great Commission on a daily basis and to live a lifestyle of peace and blessing.

TABLE OF CONTENTS

FOREWORD

What the scriptures have been telling us for over 2,000 years is now even more relevant than ever in these times of turmoil, deception and uncertainty. To best portray its powerful teachings, we must not only be "strong in the Lord," in our personal, inward dimension, but we must also learn to live in "the power of His might," the outward dimension that impacts our world.

Gail's Study Guide is the bridge between those two dimensions. This study will move you from simply acquiring internal information and inspiration to gaining external influence and bold innovation with increasing compassion. Through the applications of this challenging study, you will become a victorious change agent in our chaotic and needy world.

"Finally, be strong in the Lord and in His mighty power," that you will become **"more than a conqueror through Him who loved us."**
(See Ephesians 6:10 and Romans 8:37 NIV.)

DAVE THOMPSON
Vice President
Transform Our World

INTRODUCTION

I WELCOME YOU as you have chosen to proactively take this next step in your own quest to be "the hands and feet of Jesus." *Bravo!* I commend you for your deep desire to see this breakthrough. I am happy we can now do it together.

What you are holding is truly an extension of *His Hands, My Feet: A Journey Through the Miracles of Jesus.* Let me explain. In the origins of this work, all the material gleaned went solely into the book. There had been no thought about writing a journal. But when the Lord led us to our publisher, Michael Stickler, he wisely suggested transferring two sections of each chapter into a journal format, spurring on greater reader participation. I loved the idea! Being an avid journalist myself, my heart skipped a beat to imagine placing my own journal into your hands. Perhaps, these pages will serve as an open door to a new beginning, or a pathway to a deeper level of intimacy with Christ you've never known before.

I immediately began the work to pull out all of the "Applications" and "Observations" in each chapter. The rest of the material here evolved over the next several months. The results are purely handcrafted by listening to the Lord's leading.

As you proceed, let me encourage you to take your time. Don't simply read the book, enjoy the stories and do some busy work. Seek to commune through every page. Pray-read it. Expect the Holy Spirit to speak. Listen. Wait. Keep listening. Learn. As you commune through the applications, observations, contemplations, and meditations, do so with the same delight as taking a drink of refreshing water in the sweltering heat. **"Taste and see that the Lord is good."** (Psalms 34:8) Savor the flavors before you swallow!

The day before we shot the video for this course, the Lord enlightened me with timely insights to best prepare you for this journey.

Four issues of the heart must be addressed: they are Fear, Love, Faith and Surrender.

1. FEAR – Fear is the primary tactic of the enemy to block you from stepping out in new ways. His taunts will attempt to paralyze you, making you feel inadequate, fear looking foolish, or give in to people-pleasing. This is a *self-focused* concern about "me, myself and I." Fear says, "I can't." This means, it's time to confess fear and repent of it. Ask forgiveness for listening to the wrong voice.

2. LOVE – **"Perfect love casts out fear."** (1 John 4:18) Allow the compassion of the Lord to rise up from inside of you, to flow out with a new "people focus." Put others first. Pray for His grace to truly care about the needs of others around you.

3. FAITH – Activate faith over fear and agree with the Word. **"I can do all things through Christ who strengthens me."** (Philippians 4:13 NIV) Cancel the unbelief that God won't use you, or that you have no power to release. Put your confidence in God (residing within you)and walk in "Godfidence!"

4. SURRENDER – Make a conscious decision to yield your time each day to Him. Visualize Him in front of you, beckoning with His hand and saying, "Follow Me." I hope you will say, "Yes, Lord!"

Dealing with these four heart issues puts you in the place of grace! Now you are in position to receive His grace in the courage, boldness, and fruitfulness you desire! I am convinced you will be astounded at the new work the Lord will do in you and through you as you bless your world. Let's go!

Grow with me now and enjoy the journey!

Note: Take time to pray through those four heart issues of Fear, Love, Faith and Surrender, either alone at home or with a Facilitator in a group setting.

NOTES ON COMMUNING

If you have not begun to listen for the voice of the Lord in your journey, begin now. Confess not listening. Confess unbelief. Thank Him for His indwelling presence and His desire to speak to you.

The Lord has impressed me that "communing" is the most valuable type of prayer. It is seeking the heart of the Lord, to know Him better! This is often the most neglected type of prayer, however.

Simply cry out, *"Lord, open my ears today! Thank You! I am ready to listen!"*

As I began attempting to listen to Him several years ago, it was certainly an evolving process, but so worth the time and effort! It has been an amazing journey to learn to recognize His voice. To hear Him speak personally to me quickly took our relationship to incredible new heights.

I realized if He would speak to ME personally, He would speak to anyone else who would pursue the same.

"My sheep listen to My voice; I know them, and they follow Me." (John 10:27)

Although the Lord began to speak to me as soon as I began to ask questions, I wasn't hearing very much. In the beginning, I literally heard only *one word* a day! But that's simply what I had requested, and I felt thrilled about it!

The greater breakthrough came once I began to pick up a pen, ask a question, and wait to write His reply. He knew I was expectant (with faith, not doubt) and that whatever He would say would not be quickly forgotten.

Someone passed on a suggestion to me that someone else had just given them. It's a great question to use as a tool.

"Lord, what would You desire to say to me today?"

That brought the most incredible shift EVER in my communication with Father, Son, and Holy Spirit!

Rather than just asking a specific question for wisdom and guidance about a matter, I began to open my heart to listen to anything *He* wanted to discuss. Learning to seek

His heart in this way quickly became an *accelerated path* to enjoy a growing measure of downloads I had not yet experienced!

*I soon discovered that His favorite subject is **LOVE**!*

You, too, will be amazed at the readiness of the Lord to speak and teach you once you begin asking Him that question with pen in hand.

You will find this question incorporated in the "Communion" section of each chapter following in this journal.

Gail Okuley

Allentown, Pennsylvania

"He wakens me morning by morning,
wakens my ear to listen like one being taught."
Isaiah 50:4b

NOTE: If you need to be sure you have opened your heart to Jesus or are ready to help a friend, see "Salvation Prayer" on page 243.

NOTE ABOUT QUOTATION STYLES

1. Gail's internal dialogue: *italicized, without quotation marks.*

2. Dialogue from the Lord or the Holy Spirit with Gail: ***Bold, italicized, no quotation marks,*** when it is in God's voice.

3. Spoken dialogue from others: "In quotation marks."

4. Scripture quotations: **"Bold, in quotation marks, punctuation."** (Reference in parentheses)

"The One who enters by the gate is the Shepherd of the sheep…
and the sheep LISTEN to His voice.
…His sheep follow Him because they know His voice."
John 10:2-4 NIV

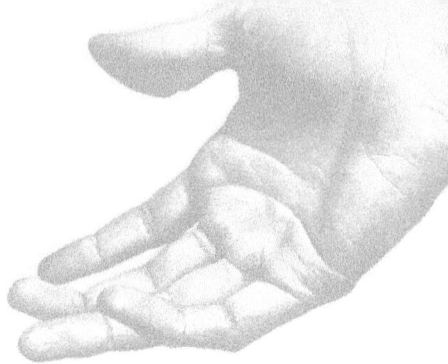

1

WATER TO WINE AT THE WEDDING

John 2:1-11

APPLICATION

Jesus' first miraculous word was: **FILL!** [Greek: *replete,* fill to the brim, or overflowing] Jesus came to pour the supernatural into the natural. He came to be emptied and poured out to fill us. *Our time has come!*

We are that blessed bride, receiving the new wine of His blood! Drink and be filled—full to overflowing! He lives within us now in His full resurrection power. It is our privilege and responsibility now to serve Him with that God-given supernatural power and to respond obediently as those humble servants did to Mary's instructions: **"Whatever He says to you, do it!"** (John 2:5)

OBSERVATIONS OF THE BIBLICAL ACCOUNT

1. John 2:1 begins with **"On the third day."** This timing amplifies the prophetic significance of the entire miracle. In the resurrection, His earthen vessel became glorified on the third day, just as water became wine, representing the blood of Jesus.

2. How significant it is that the first blessing from His hands was reserved for a **bride,** though she knew it not. Today, we are that blessed bride, receiving the new wine of His blood!

3. Another symbolic fact to note is the **six stone pots**: the number six represents man, and stone can represent our earthen vessels. He provided enough new wine to fill ALL the earthen vessels of mankind.

COMMUNION

Open my heart, Holy Spirit, to be still and listen to Your heart. Help me to receive and believe. Prepare me for powerful new activation.

Biblical Applications and Observations

_____

_____

_____

_____

_____

_____

_____

_____

_____

_____

_____

ALONG THE WAY Reflections (on the author's story)

_____

_____

_____

_____

_____

_____

_____

_____

_____

_____

_____

_____

CONTEMPLATIONS

When did I receive the new wine of His spirit?

When have I responded to His voice lately?

What supernatural works of the Lord have I observed in recent weeks?

Contemplations Response

_____

_____

_____

_____

_____

_____

_____

_____

_____

_____

_____

Lord, what would You desire to say to me today?

_____

_____

_____

_____

_____

_____

_____

_____

_____

_____

_____

ACTIVATION PRAYER

Lord, I receive the new wine You desire for me! Help me to press in close to Your heart and follow You passionately. Empower me to be Your hands and feet, to pour out Your lavish love and grace for others. I yield fully to your Holy Spirit. Release Your miraculous power through me today!

MY "ALONG THE WAY" STORIES

Keep this journal ready to fill in your stories when they happen!

"He who says he abides in Him ought...to WALK JUST AS HE WALKED."
1 John 2:6

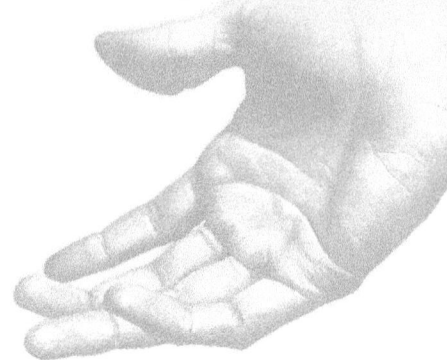

2

"UNCLEAN SPIRIT" IN THE SYNAGOGUE

Mark 1:21-28, Luke 4:31-37

APPLICATION

As Jesus pointedly reminded me that I, and all His believers, are now His temple, He led me to revisit this miracle account and place His visit to the temple in the context of my heart. Jesus went to the cross: I met Him there long ago and invited Him into my life. Immediately He came inside! **"Or do you not know that your body is the temple of the Holy Spirit who is in you, whom you have from God, and you are not your own?"** (1 Corinthians 6:19)

He came inside as my Lord and Master, residing here in this temple, to transform my life daily. The greatest Teacher of all speaks to me— **"Learn from Me, for I am gentle and humble."** (Matthew 11:29)

"Then the Lord reached out his hand and touched my mouth and said to me, I have put my words in your mouth." (Jeremiah 1:9) **"Behold, I give you the authority to trample on serpents and scorpions, and over all the power of the enemy, and nothing shall by any means hurt you."** (Luke 10:19)

As I willingly open my mouth and release His truth and light, people will be astonished at the authority and power of His Spirit seen and heard in this holy temple. I must make no unholy alliances with the enemy and allow him any space within me, my thoughts, my will, or my emotions. My spirit must submit to His Spirit to allow Him to have full authority over my flesh. **"Whoever wants to be my disciple must deny** themselves and take up their cross daily and follow me." (Luke 9:23) Miracles will flow from the unhindered residence of "His Holiness" in my temple!

OBSERVATIONS OF THE BIBLICAL ACCOUNT

1. The Spirit **finally** drew Jesus to go to the synagogue to speak the truth! The Lord's time to speak out had come. **"Zeal for His Father's house consumed Him."** (Psalms 69:9)

2. The Father allowed a startling **disruption** to visually demonstrate the truth of His teaching: new power and authority no one had seen or heard before.

"Then the Lord reached out his hand and
touched my mouth and said to me,
I have put my words in your mouth."
Jeremiah 1:9

COMMUNION

Open my heart, Holy Spirit, to be still and listen to Your heart. Help me to receive and believe. Prepare me for powerful new activation.

Biblical Applications and Observations

_____

_____

_____

_____

_____

_____

_____

_____

_____

_____

_____

_____

_____

ALONG THE WAY Reflections (on the author's story)

_____

_____

_____

_____

_____

_____

_____

_____

_____

_____

_____

_____

CONTEMPLATIONS

How do I keep my temple cleansed for a holy resting place for His Spirit?

Lord, how can you use my life to help draw others into freedom?

Lord, please identify any unclean habits that have become open doors to the enemy.

Contemplations Response

_____

_____

_____

_____

_____

_____

_____

_____

_____

_____

_____

_____

Lord, what would You desire to say to me today?

_____

_____

_____

_____

_____

_____

_____

_____

_____

_____

ACTIVATION PRAYER

Cleanse my temple, Lord, by your perfect love. Open my eyes to see what you see. Have your way, Your Holiness! Fill up this vessel with Your light! I choose to walk in complete freedom to set others free in the world around me, as You lead me, in the Name of Jesus!

MY "ALONG THE WAY" STORIES

Keep this journal ready to fill in your stories when they happen!

_____

_____

_____

_____

_____

_____

_____

_____

_____

_____

_____

_____

_____

_____

_____

_____

_____

_____

_____

"He who says he abides in Him ought…to WALK JUST AS HE WALKED."
1 John 2:6

"The Spirit of the LORD is on ME,
because the Lord has anointed ME
to proclaim good news to the poor.
He has sent ME to bind up the brokenhearted,
to proclaim FREEDOM for the captives
and release from darkness
for the prisoners."

Isaiah 61:1 NIV
(emphasis added)

This is true for every follower of Jesus!

3

REBUKING THE FEVER

Matthew 8:14-17, Mark 1:29-31, Luke 4:38-39

APPLICATION

The Lord certainly desires His healing power to flow in our homes, as well as elsewhere. He wants to be invited there, into our homes, to do what only He can do.

Even if most of the family members are unsaved, the Lord's new entry point into a family can be through any trial through His supernatural intervention. Young or old, people become desperate and open when they are sick.

"What the enemy intends for evil, God intends for good."

(See Genesis 50:20)

"They overcame by the blood of the Lamb, and the word of their testimony."
(Revelation 12:11)

Speaking His word is a powerful way to see healing come forth.

OBSERVATIONS

1. The woman's fever had clearly come from the **enemy**, as He had to rebuke it! Once restored, she immediately chose to serve Him!

2. In my home it's interesting that He intervened dramatically in two of our young sons several years before He brought my healing. The **timing** of the Lord is quite unpredictable.

COMMUNION

Open my heart, Holy Spirit, to be still and listen to Your heart. Help me to receive and believe. Prepare me for powerful new activation.

Biblical Applications and Observations

_____

_____

_____

_____

_____

_____

_____

_____

_____

_____

_____

_____

ALONG THE WAY Reflections (on the author's story)

_____

_____

_____

_____

_____

_____

_____

_____

_____

_____

_____

_____

CONTEMPLATIONS

How does my family see the love and peace of Jesus in my life?

How have I been His healing agent in our home?

How have I learned to exercise my authority in the Name of Jesus?

Contemplations Response

_____

_____

_____

_____

_____

_____

_____

_____

_____

_____

_____

Lord, what would You desire to say to me today?

_____

_____

_____

_____

_____

_____

_____

_____

_____

_____

_____

_____

ACTIVATION PRAYER

Lord grant me the readiness to listen, hear, obey and be a healing agent at home. May 'the God of peace crush the enemy' under my feet (Romans 16:20) inside and outside the walls of my home. Lead me in compassion to help the sick arise in the name of Jesus, even today.

MY "ALONG THE WAY" STORIES

Keep this journal ready to fill in your stories when they happen!

"He who says he abides in Him ought...to WALK JUST AS HE WALKED."
1 John 2:6

A DECREE OUT OF SICKNESS:

UP, up, up, out of the pit of weakness and sickness, I will now ARISE, in Jesus Name.

Your Kingdom come! Your will be done in this earthen vessel, as it is in heaven!

I bless my spirit to dominate over my flesh in complete ALIGNMENT with heaven, according to your word in Philippians 3:20, that I am now a citizen of heaven.

Behold! You are doing a new thing in me today.

Today I am breaking agreement with old mindsets of weakness of the flesh and aligning fully with my complete RESTORATION, as in the beginning, before the fall of man.

Thank you for taking the curse of sickness and disease upon Yourself for me (Galatians 3:13). I now appropriate my freedom.

Thank you for being the lifter of my head.

The OLD must GO, and the NEW must COME!

I believe. I receive my blessings of grace, grace, grace.

No weapons of sickness formed against me shall prosper.

I am now free to rise UP on wings of eagles—to walk and not grow weary, to run and not faint, to soar high and higher in the power of Your Spirit.

I have fixed my eyes upon You, Lord Jesus, as my Deliverer.

This daughter/son has cried out and you have heard my plea and delivered me from all my troubles. (Psalm 34:6)

Prince of Peace, reign here in my body, soul, spirit.

The God of Peace shall now crush the enemy of LIFE underneath my feet.

Hallelujah! Victory is mine!

THANK YOU! As I decree a thing, it shall be established. (Job 22:28)

Anything else Lord?

Praise Me! Praise Me in the storm.

Let no unwholesome words proceed out of your mouth, only praise!

Rejoice always!

Thank you, Lord, the victory is won. IT IS FINISHED!

Let's rise up and walk in our God-give authority over sickness, starting with our own bodies! We can and we must! As we do so for ourselves, we will have even greater faith to do so for others.

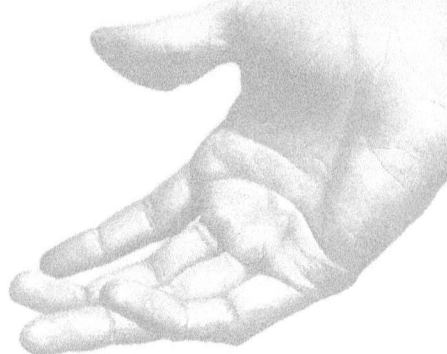

4

CITY SEEKS JESUS AT PETER'S HOUSE

Matthew 8:16-17, Mark 1:32-34, Luke 4:40-41

APPLICATION

Jesus waited thirty years for the Father to release Him and His miraculous power. We must trust Him in our journey of preparation. Only He knows when He will choose to pour out His power through us. The key is to walk in love and compassion. Many testify that they prayed for many before the first one received their healing. When He compels us to do so, they are still touched by our love.

As we gain His heart of compassion, we will begin to pray for miracles everywhere we go. When His power breaks out through our hands and feet, it may only take two or three miracles for the world to come knocking at our doors.

"Not by might, nor by power, but by My Spirit,' says the Lord." (Zechariah 4:6)

OBSERVATIONS OF THE BIBLICAL ACCOUNT

1. When He knocks on a new door for us, the whole trajectory of our future can **shift** in a moment. He has prepared us for things we know not.

2. It **only took two** public miracles to bring the whole city seeking Jesus.

COMMUNION

Open my heart, Holy Spirit, to be still and listen to Your heart. Help me to receive and believe. Prepare me for powerful new activation.

Biblical Applications and Observations

ALONG THE WAY Reflections (on the author's story)

CONTEMPLATIONS

How can I more freely open my door to the world?

How should I adjust my actions, to give the Lord complete freedom in my life?

Am I ready for His "suddenlys," to bring the multitudes to me?

Contemplations Response

_____

_____

_____

_____

_____

_____

_____

_____

_____

_____

_____

Lord, what would You desire to say to me today?

_____

_____

_____

_____

_____

_____

_____

_____

_____

_____

ACTIVATION PRAYER

*Lord, prepare my heart for Your amazing suddenlys. Give me ears to hear the cries of the sick and wounded! Heal the masses through my hands, this day, this week, this year. Release Your supernatural power **now** into my life!*

MY "ALONG THE WAY" STORIES

Keep this journal ready to fill in your stories when they happen!

"He who says he abides in Him ought...to WALK JUST AS HE WALKED."
1 John 2:6

5

MIRACULOUS CATCH OF FISH

Luke 5:1-11

APPLICATION

When Jesus climbs into *our boat* in the midst of our lives (salvation), we have invited Him to come. Yet do we recognize that Wisdom has come to join us and lead us in a new Way of life? We probably didn't in the beginning, especially if we met Him in our childhood. Yet, now as adults, have we embraced His Way for today, tomorrow, and the next?

Why do we not expect the supernatural to invade our boat today?! He knows us all too well. He knows it often takes many years of toilsome weariness to no avail before we will cast Him a furtive look and finally yield to His plan. In our ultimate depths of weariness, He will challenge us—*"Go back out!"*

We must go on pure faith then. Nothing in us will want to do it. We must go out and discover the depths of what only He can do! At times, He likewise asks us to leave our nets at the height of success, as with Simon after the great catch. At other times, His great call will be simply to remain in the marketplace and shine His supernatural Light there.

Strengthen us, Lord, to pull in those nets (together) that are about to break!

---

*Why do we not expect the supernatural
to invade our boat today?!*

OBSERVATIONS OF THE BIBLICAL ACCOUNT

1. What an amazing **turn of events**! So unassuming were the actions of the Lord, as He climbed into the boat, and asked His small favor! Yet, the very thing that may have tempted them to go back out—hoping to catch more fish—instead opened the eyes of their hearts to the greater blessing: the Man JESUS! They heard the Voice of purpose and destiny calling and they said, "YES!" Jesus had climbed into the boat alone, but He climbed out with four new followers! *When the Lord asks a favor, His favor will return to us.* We cannot out give God!

2. Matthew 4 and Mark 1 both relate the call to *"Follow Me,"* but surprisingly did not relate the **miraculous catch** of fish!

Follow Me!
There was a choice and a calling made by the Father,
for these ordinary, unqualified men to follow Me,
who would soon become world changers.

COMMUNION

Open my heart, Holy Spirit, to be still and listen to Your heart. Help me to receive and believe. Prepare me for powerful new activation.

Biblical Applications and Observations

_____

_____

_____

_____

_____

_____

_____

_____

_____

_____

_____

_____

ALONG THE WAY Reflections (on the author's story)

_____

_____

_____

_____

_____

_____

_____

_____

_____

_____

_____

CONTEMPLATIONS

Am I willing to get out of my boat? Who owns my boat?

How or where do I expect to see the miraculous today?

What fears are stopping me today from following Him or doing the 'new?'

Contemplations Response

_____

_____

_____

_____

_____

_____

_____

_____

_____

_____

_____

_____

Lord, what would You desire to say to me today?

_____

_____

_____

_____

_____

_____

_____

_____

_____

_____

_____

_____

ACTIVATION PRAYER

Lord, open my ears and eyes daily to listen well, and to see where Your footprints are leading. I yield it all to You. Refresh my heart with a growing expectation for greatness as Your disciple. Thank You for Your faithfulness to provide in ways that are beyond comprehension.

MY "ALONG THE WAY" STORIES

Keep this journal ready to fill in your stories when they happen!

_____

_____

_____

_____

_____

_____

_____

_____

_____

_____

_____

_____

_____

_____

_____

_____

_____

_____

_____

"He who says he abides in Him ought...to WALK JUST AS HE WALKED."
1 John 2:6

FURTHER MEDITATION: FOLLOW ME

Have you heard this call? What and when was your first call to come to Him?

_____

_____

_____

Write a brief testimony of your salvation decision.

_____

_____

_____

_____

_____

Describe subsequent times when He has called you out of something familiar, and into the new!

_____

_____

Where do you sense that He wants you to be in your journey? In your career? In your free time?

_____

_____

How is He calling you NOW to follow Him in a new way?

_____

_____

_____

What must you do now to get out of the old familiar boat to answer His call?

_____

_____

_____

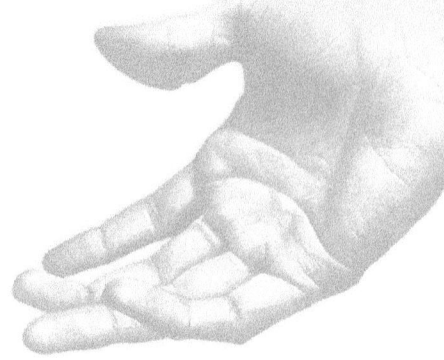

6

HEALING THE LEPER

Matthew 8:1- 4, Mark 1:40-45, Luke 5:12-14

APPLICATION

So should we expect to see and hear from Him what we are to do—miracles amidst our daily lives! In my journaling a few years ago, the Lord was speaking on His favorite subject again: *Love.*

"A decision to not choose love is the worst decision anyone can make.

Choose love. Stop choosing whom to love.

Let Me choose whom—I choose the world!"

Only the *hands and feet of Jesus* today can bring love, supernatural grace and power into their hopelessness.

Then He said to them, *"Whoever wants to be My disciple must deny themselves and take up their cross daily and follow Me."* (Luke 9:23)

It's time to love the unlovely. It's time to be the voice of hope.

OBSERVATIONS OF THE BIBLICAL ACCOUNT

1. Jesus always had time for the **least of these.**

2. Despite the power being released through Him, He wisely relied on His ongoing prayer interaction with the **Father.** He did not try to be self-sufficient, to decide what to do, or when. He relied fully on the Father. Then He could be confident the breakthrough had already been accomplished.

COMMUNION

Open my heart, Holy Spirit, to be still and listen to Your heart. Help me to receive and believe. Prepare me for powerful new activation.

Biblical Applications and Observations

_____

_____

_____

_____

_____

_____

_____

_____

_____

_____

_____

ALONG THE WAY Reflections (on the author's story)

_____

_____

_____

_____

_____

_____

_____

_____

_____

_____

_____

_____

_____

CONTEMPLATIONS

How can I better connect with those the world rejects?
Do I willingly approach the unclean, with Love in my eyes?
Will I learn to ask the Father what to do and say?

Contemplations Response

_____

_____

_____

_____

_____

_____

_____

_____

_____

_____

_____

_____

Lord, what would You desire to say to me today?

_____

_____

_____

_____

_____

_____

_____

_____

_____

_____

_____

_____

_____

ACTIVATION PRAYER

Lord, cleanse my heart and my hands each day. Open my heart to expand and believe things I never thought possible. Use my clean hands to touch the unclean with the power of the blood of Jesus and see unbelievable transformations all along the way!

MY "ALONG THE WAY" STORIES

Keep this journal ready to fill in your stories when they happen!

"He who says he abides in Him ought...to WALK JUST AS HE WALKED."
1 John 2:6

7

PARALYTIC LOWERED THROUGH THE ROOF

Matthew 9:1-8, Mark 2:1-12, Luke 5:17-26

APPLICATION

To be forgiven is to be free and stand tall! *Rise up and walk!*
"He whom the son sets free, is free indeed!" (John 8:36 my paraphrase)

"It is for freedom that Christ has set us free. Stand firm, then, and do not let yourselves be burdened again by a yoke of slavery." (Galatians 5:1 NIV)

As believers, we are free. Apart from the power of Jesus, there is no freedom. (See page 53.) Hindrances of old habits and mindsets must go! We must break agreement with old mindsets that rob us of life. It is only in believing the lie of the enemy that we are not free, that bondage remains.

As free men and women let's bring others to meet Him for healing and freedom, no matter what the cost. Let's ignore ridicule when we know the right thing to do.

When we recognize the power of the Lord present to touch others, let's be His ready vessel.

"He who the son sets free, is free indeed!"
John 8:36 my paraphrase

OBSERVATIONS OF THE BIBLICAL ACCOUNT

1. The religious leaders were trying to **dissect** the supernatural through the natural or dilute the supernatural to their own understanding. They were trying to put God in the proverbial box, instead of letting the supernatural take the lid off the box. They considered His authority to be ludicrous audacity and false!

    (Let's not consider His authority as *nothing* in us!)

2. They seemed paralyzed and **powerless** in the darkness of their fear and unbelief.

He received the paralytic eagerly,
not as an intrusion,
but happily and compassionately.
The BLESSING went beyond the request,
not just physical healing, but a healing of the heart.

COMMUNION

Open my heart, Holy Spirit, to be still and listen to Your heart. Help me to receive and believe. Prepare me for powerful new activation.

Biblical Applications and Observations

_____

_____

_____

_____

_____

_____

_____

_____

_____

_____

ALONG THE WAY Reflections (on the author's story)

_____

_____

_____

_____

_____

_____

_____

_____

_____

_____

_____

CONTEMPLATIONS

Am I free? Have I forgiven myself?

What yokes of slavery am I still carrying that the Lord already took for me?

How can I better prepare to do the next thing He asks of me, outside my comfort zone?

Contemplations Response

Lord, what would You desire to say to me today?

ACTIVATION PRAYER

Lord, grant me discernment to know how to carry my friends to YOU to be healed by Your great love! Thank you for Your priceless gift of Love You have for each one of us. Help me to yield to others when it is my own time to be carried, Lord. Thank You for Your healing power and that **"with God, all things are possible!"** *(Matthew 19:26 NIV)*

MY "ALONG THE WAY" STORIES

Keep this journal ready to fill in your stories when they happen!

_____

_____

_____

_____

_____

_____

_____

_____

_____

_____

_____

_____

_____

_____

_____

_____

_____

_____

_____

_____

_____

"He who says he abides in Him ought...to WALK JUST AS HE WALKED."
1 John 2:6

FURTHER MEDITATION: FREEDOM

"It is for freedom that Christ has set us free. Stand firm, then, and do not let yourselves be burdened again by a yoke of slavery." (Galatians 5:1 NIV)

I'll share a brief testimony here. Several years ago, when the Lord first highlighted this verse to me, He interrupted my reading with, ***Are you free?***

I didn't know what to say. I had never felt free, as I knew several areas that could easily defeat me.

But I knew what I just read in this verse.

I don't know, Lord.

Are you free? He persisted a second time.

I don't feel fully free yet, though this verse says I already am.

Are you free? He wouldn't let me miss this.

I said nothing.

Just say it, He said.

I hesitated, but obedience spoke the words for me: *I'm free.*

Oh! As soon as the words came out of my mouth, the reality of the truth penetrated deeply so I could actually believe it!

Wow, I'm FREE!

I had never known!

That old devil, that liar! He really had me fooled.

So, who are we agreeing with?

If there are pet sins you enjoy, it's time to choose to let them go, confess them and choose HIs way to live. Freedom is yours.

Just say it!

Thank you, Lord, for setting me free. I am free!

8

HEALING A MAN'S HAND ON THE SABBATH

Matthew 12:8-14, Mark 2:27–3:6, Luke 6:5-11

APPLICATION

What would happen in our houses of worship if the Lord interrupted our "order of service" with a miraculous healing?

Do we have openness or fearfulness to His Spirit working?

I am reminded of Jesus speaking to the church of Laodicea "...**be earnest and repent. Here I am! I stand at the door and knock. If anyone hears my voice and opens the door, I will come in and eat with them, and they with me.**" (Revelation 3:19-20)

We must be careful to re-examine our own traditions and modes of operation periodically, to line up with His desire to adjust us when needed.

We must be careful not to overrule His power that should constantly be working in unexpected ways.

OBSERVATIONS

1. We know that Jesus only did what the Father showed Him. Obviously, the Lord needed to break down the **Sabbath** rules that had become overbearing and overly legalistic. God's timing is always precise and intentional.
   (*The miracles of chapters 31 and 34 describe others done on the Sabbath.*)

2. In Jesus' perfection, He could be both **angered and grieved** for the Pharisees' hearts.

COMMUNION

Open my heart, Holy Spirit, to be still and listen to Your heart. Help me to receive and believe. Prepare me for powerful new activation.

Biblical Applications and Observations

_____

_____

_____

_____

_____

_____

_____

_____

_____

_____

_____

_____

_____

ALONG THE WAY Reflections (on the author's story)

_____

_____

_____

_____

_____

_____

_____

_____

_____

_____

_____

_____

CONTEMPLATIONS

What limitations have I placed on my faith?
How could I allow love and compassion to rule my day?
What impossibility do you want me to pray for today, Lord?

Contemplations Response

Lord, what would You desire to say to me today?

ACTIVATION PRAYER

Use me Lord to become Your hands and feet for healing miracles, with courage, kindness, faith and the "dunamis" (dynamite power) of the Spirit! Overrule any old fearful mindsets to let You touch others through me. Increase my boldness when all eyes are upon me!

MY "ALONG THE WAY" STORIES

Keep this journal ready to fill in your stories when they happen!

"He who says he abides in Him ought...to WALK JUST AS HE WALKED."
1 John 2:6

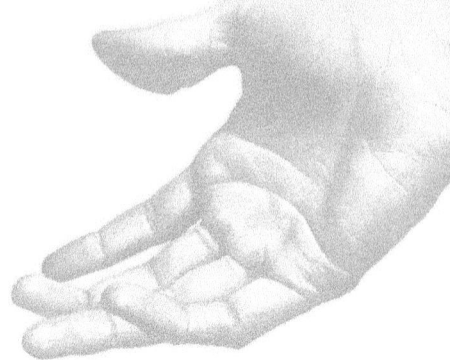

9

HEALING A GREAT MULTITUDE

Matthew 12:15-16, Mark 3:7-12, Luke 6:17-19

APPLICATION

God uses **"all things together for good."** (Romans 8:28) The rejection in the temple from just one healing sent Jesus out in the streets where the multitudes were, and ironically where healing could flow freely!

How have we missed this?

I have often thought about God's plan to send Jesus to earth at that time, in the age where He had to walk everywhere—not passing people by quickly as we do in this age of autos, planes, and trains. He could practically make strong eye contact with most everyone *along the way.*

Unlike today, however, communication would have been very limited across the miles. Yet how quickly this word-of-mouth wildfire had spread to the surrounding regions— still quite early in His ministry. *We must slow down for people! We must see them, hear them, and touch them.*

We have erred long enough in coldly ignoring people surrounding us along the way. In some regions and countries this is far worse than others. We must be praying to learn to engage at least some of the people around us with a godly heart connection of His love.

OBSERVATIONS OF THE BIBLICAL ACCOUNT

1. Though the enemy could not help but identify Jesus in the power confrontations, He surprisingly chose not to receive any honor from the enemy's camp! It is amazing to realize, however, that demons had **no option** but to submit to the Lord!

2. As Jesus walked **along the way**, Love flowed openly and visibly, so that word spread excitedly, far and wide, by word of mouth. How powerful were His words of Life and the testimonies of others that sparked new hope and faith!

*"At the name of Jesus every knee should bow...
and every tongue should confess that
JESUS CHRIST IS LORD!"
Philippians 2:10-11*

COMMUNION

Open my heart, Holy Spirit, to be still and listen to Your heart. Help me to receive and believe. Prepare me for powerful new activation.

Biblical Applications and Observations

_____

_____

_____

_____

_____

_____

_____

_____

_____

_____

_____

ALONG THE WAY Reflections (on the author's story)

_____

_____

_____

_____

_____

_____

_____

_____

_____

_____

CONTEMPLATIONS

How do I need to grow my faith that You will heal my own body, Lord?

Lord, will you grant me a new vision for myself, to walk in greater power?

Will You heal the multitudes through these hands, Lord?

Contemplations Response

_____

_____

_____

_____

_____

_____

_____

_____

_____

_____

_____

Lord, what would You desire to say to me today?

_____

_____

_____

_____

_____

_____

_____

_____

_____

_____

_____

ACTIVATION PRAYER

Lord, I receive new vision from You, to see the people You place in my path every day, to touch with Your kindness, love, and power. I choose to operate in the ongoing revelation of the resurrected Christ dwelling within me. Use me as Your anointed vessel today, wherever I go! Open my ears to hear the silent cries of the multitudes living in despair.

MY "ALONG THE WAY" STORIES

Keep this journal ready to fill in your stories when they happen!

_____

_____

_____

_____

_____

_____

_____

_____

_____

_____

_____

_____

_____

_____

_____

_____

_____

_____

_____

_____

"He who says he abides in Him ought...to WALK JUST AS HE WALKED."
1 John 2:6

He had come to love,
to bless, to teach, to train, to restore.

Heaven had come down to earth.

No one was turned away.
Love had come and had come for a great purpose.

10

CENTURION'S SERVANT NEAR DEATH

(Matthew 8:5-13), Luke 7:1-10

APPLICATION

Humility. Honor.
Compassion. Desperate faith.

Sacrifice. Hope.

Dire pursuit of Jesus. These are to be our life traits as His hands and feet.

When we find ourselves feeling alone, we must know our Comforter walks with us, as our **"ever present help."** (Psalms 46:1) Every believing family member has the Healer resident within, to carry them and restore them, though we may be far away. Our hope must remain in Him, not what man can do. Our faith and our prayers are enough to move mountains, even if we cannot be present.

OBSERVATIONS OF THE BIBLICAL ACCOUNT

1. Jesus did not have to be physically present for healing—much like today! How He wants to **confidently** operate through us like this in prayer!

2. Interestingly, it was a Roman stranger who was commended with such great faith, not a disciple. He was likely a newer believer than the disciples themselves. Despite widespread Jewish resistance to Rome's presence there, Jesus' compassion knew no barriers towards 'unwelcome' **foreigners**.

3. How precious is the great **humility** in this officer's heart, to serve his servant with such great love and compassion, giving of his own time, energy, and reputation.

COMMUNION

Open my heart, Holy Spirit, to be still and listen to Your heart. Help me to receive and believe. Prepare me for powerful new activation.

Biblical Applications and Observations

_____

_____

_____

_____

_____

_____

_____

_____

_____

_____

_____

_____

_____

ALONG THE WAY Reflections (on the author's story)

_____

_____

_____

_____

_____

_____

_____

_____

_____

_____

_____

_____

CONTEMPLATIONS

How desperate is my faith?

What kind of barriers do I have in my heart toward any foreigners?

How can I trust Jesus more fully with the life of a dear one who is suffering?

Contemplations Response

_____

_____

_____

_____

_____

_____

_____

_____

_____

_____

_____

_____

_____

Lord, what would You desire to say to me today?

_____

_____

_____

_____

_____

_____

_____

_____

_____

_____

ACTIVATION PRAYER

Oh Lord, my eyes are upon You as Jehovah Rapha, God the Healer. Strengthen my heart to believe You in each desperate trial, whether mine or that of others. Increase the boldness of my faith, so that when You look over my life and my city, You will smile and say—

Such great faith I have not seen as this, in all the land!

MY "ALONG THE WAY" STORIES

Keep this journal ready to fill in your stories when they happen!

_____

_____

_____

_____

_____

_____

_____

_____

_____

_____

_____

_____

_____

_____

_____

_____

_____

"He who says he abides in Him ought...to WALK JUST AS HE WALKED."
1 John 2:6

11

RESURRECTION: A WIDOW'S SON

Luke 7:11-17

APPLICATION

It's never too late for God.

In the most hopeless situations, we are to look to Jesus!

Let's gain more sensitivity to be in the right place at the right time, like Jesus that day. No one expected the funeral to end without a body!

I didn't know when I began praying some strange prayers by myself at a creek every week that the Lord had planned such BIG ripples for me to see over time, impacting hundreds of lives. *We cannot go by what we see and feel.* I felt small and hidden. But He took quiet simple prayers and produced life there at our Jordan, in ways I never dreamed.

Let's rise to the occasion, whether big or small. We never know what God will do through our small acts of obedience. We may be the ones He will use to release resurrection glory one day.

OBSERVATIONS OF THE BIBLICAL ACCOUNT

1. Jesus wisely placed **His hand** only on the coffin, not on the boy, thus He had not become unclean. *The glory of God touched the boy's corpse, nonetheless!*

2. Perhaps the miracle the **day before** (the centurion's servant) helped prepare Jesus for this next step, of manifesting His power beyond the gates of death. Only a few breaths separated the two miracles.

COMMUNION

Open my heart, Holy Spirit, to be still and listen to Your heart. Help me to receive and believe. Prepare me for powerful new activation.

Biblical Applications and Observations

_____

_____

_____

_____

_____

_____

_____

_____

_____

_____

_____

_____

ALONG THE WAY Reflections (on the author's story)

_____

_____

_____

_____

_____

_____

_____

_____

_____

_____

_____

_____

CONTEMPLATIONS

Lord, how can I better yield my free time, to be led by You?

Will you open my eyes to see people the way you see them, Lord?

How does my faith need to shift, to see the dead arise?

Contemplations Response

_____

_____

_____

_____

_____

_____

_____

_____

_____

_____

_____

_____

_____

_____

Lord, what would You desire to say to me today?

_____

_____

_____

_____

_____

_____

_____

_____

_____

_____

_____

ACTIVATION PRAYER

Saturate me with the power of Your light, life and love with 'more than enough' to release into the pain and trauma surrounding me in the world. Thank you, God, that You want to pour out everlasting life through my life to even raise the dead! My life is Yours Lord. **Nothing is too hard for You.** *Here I am. Use me.*

MY "ALONG THE WAY" STORIES

Keep this journal ready to fill in your stories when they happen!

"He who says he abides in Him ought...to WALK JUST AS HE WALKED."
1 John 2:6

12

NOBLEMAN'S SON RESTORED

John 4:46-54

APPLICATION

We must live and die with **faith**, **hope** and **love** stamped firmly upon our hearts, minds and spirits. **"Nothing is too hard for the Lord!"** (Jeremiah 32:17) We must never give up. His plan was and is to bring ALL into the fold, for "household salvation." **"Believe in the Lord Jesus, and you will be saved—you and your household."** (Acts 1:31) To believe means to be fully persuaded.

"The Lord is not slack concerning His promise. . .but is longsuffering toward us, not willing that any should perish but that all should come to repentance." (2 Peter 3:9)

When we are personally walking in relationship with Jesus, with part of our family unbelieving, we need to petition the Lord expectantly on their behalf, and make His presence known through us, to minister His Perfect Love in our household. We should literally open the front door of our house and invite the presence of the Lord Jesus to come in and fill the house as Savior, Healer, and our great Peacemaker!

When there is no freedom to pray about anything with family members, there is still a way to minister. We are to bless them in our hearts with unconditional love, peace and grace. We must not harbor frustration and resentment.

The Lord will grow new life from our faithful plantings of faith, hope, and love.

OBSERVATIONS OF THE BIBLICAL ACCOUNT

1. **Three** people dying, three days, apparently in this chronological order. Jesus later died as one of three, hanging between two thieves, and rose in three days. God often seems to carefully place His numbers in alignment!

2. Faith was in the air, at this place of His first miracle, turning water into wine. This account was the first mention of many passages regarding **"household salvation."**

3. Even though the Lord spoke a rebuke, the **desperate faith**, hope and love of the father would not be deterred.

"Sir, come!" he insisted! He spoke his confident faith against all odds, despite the discouraging words from Jesus. *Faith, hope and love won!*

We must live and die
*with **faith**, **hope** and **love** stamped firmly*
upon our hearts, minds and spirits.
We must never give up.

COMMUNION

Open my heart, Holy Spirit, to be still and listen to Your heart. Help me to receive and believe. Prepare me for powerful new activation.

Biblical Applications and Observations

_____

_____

_____

_____

_____

_____

_____

_____

_____

_____

_____

_____

ALONG THE WAY Reflections (on the author's story)

_____

_____

_____

_____

_____

_____

_____

_____

_____

_____

_____

CONTEMPLATIONS

How do I guard my faith, hope and love to stay firmly rooted in all situations?

When has the Lord put a demand on my faith, and how did I respond?

Am I believing God for the salvation of my entire household, as He has promised?

Contemplations Response

Lord, what would You desire to say to me today?

ACTIVATION PRAYER

Oh God, stir up great faith in my heart that will not falter, as well as great confidence in Your heart of love in place of fear, doubt or hopelessness. Help me, Father, to continuously keep the fires of faith, love and passion burning brightly in my heart, to draw others to the Light. Use me powerfully in my home, Lord, for 'household salvation.'

MY "ALONG THE WAY" STORIES

Keep this journal ready to fill in your stories when they happen!

"He who says he abides in Him ought...to WALK JUST AS HE WALKED."
1 John 2:6

FURTHER MEDITATION: HOUSEHOLD SALVATION

Be encouraged as you pray and believe for salvation and breakthroughs in your household.

Keep in mind that the Greek word for salvation is SOZO, which means healed, whole, and delivered; in body, soul and spirit. It's far beyond simply the forgiveness of sins.

Consider these words of encouragement in the New Testament:

"Call for Simon. . . who will tell you words by which you and all your household will be saved." (Acts 11:13-14)

"So they said, "Believe on the Lord Jesus, and you will be saved, you and your household." (Acts 16:31)

"For the unbelieving husband is sanctified by the wife, and the unbelieving wife is sanctified by her husband." (1 Corinthians 7:14)

"And he himself believed, and his whole household." (John 4:53)

"Now this is the confidence that we have in Him, that if we ask anything according to His will, He hears us." (1 John 5:14)

"The Lord is not slack concerning His promise. . . not willing that any should perish but that ALL should come to repentance." (2 Peter 3:9)

"Let us then approach God's throne of grace with confidence, so that we may receive mercy and find grace to help us in our time of need." (Hebrews 4:16 NIV)

For all the promises of God in Him are YES, and in Him, AMEN, to the glory of God through us. (2 Corinthians 1:20)

*For great encouragement in praying for the salvation of a family member, watch this movie, an amazing true story: **The Perfect Wave** (2014), about Ian McCormack, a New Zealand surfer and atheist who had a near death experience and returned. (www.theperfectwave.co.za)*

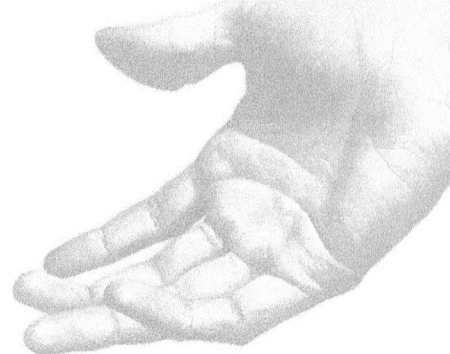

13

CASTING OUT A BLIND MUTE DEMON

Matthew 12:22-30, (Mark 3:20-27), Luke 11:14-20

APPLICATION

We must give no room for division, except to "divide the spoils" of the enemy! WE have the upper Hand!

"The God of peace will soon crush satan underneath your feet." (Romans 16:20)

The Prince of Peace desires to do so, and equipped us with shoes "shod with peace," according to Ephesians 6:15. We must therefore take His peace wherever we go.

> *The Lord spoke to me once that we are to*
>
> ***"walk crushing the enemy under our feet"***
>
> *on a daily basis.*

Our place is UP in victory, and the devil's place is DOWN under our feet!

We are to fear not, but to walk and grow in bold confidence in our authority in Jesus Name, knowing that *He always leads us in triumph*, according to 2 Corinthians 2:14.

We are not to allow the enemy to mute our own voices in shyness, timidity, fear or insecurity. This denotes a self-focus. We are to open our mouths wide and let the Lord fill it, with blessings and affirmations of others around us, thinking of others more than ourselves.

OBSERVATIONS OF THE BIBLICAL ACCOUNT

1. As the Light came to give Life, the enemy still tried to take the credit and receive glory unto himself (through the dark comments of the Pharisees) just as he had done in heaven before being cast out. How ridiculous were those comments; the religious leaders were clearly **duped** into speaking so foolishly.

2. The **Lord knows** precisely what we need, whether physical, spiritual, emotional, social, or economic. Courage and perseverance may be a greater need than sight or hearing.

"The God of peace
will soon crush satan
*underneath **your** feet."*
Romans 16:20

COMMUNION

Open my heart, Holy Spirit, to be still and listen to Your heart. Help me to receive and believe. Prepare me for powerful new activation.

Biblical Applications and Observations

_____

_____

_____

_____

_____

_____

_____

_____

_____

_____

_____

_____

ALONG THE WAY Reflections (on the author's story)

_____

_____

_____

_____

_____

_____

_____

_____

_____

_____

_____

_____

CONTEMPLATIONS

How well has my faith persevered while seeing no breakthroughs?

How can I grow my confidence when negativity spirals around me?

How can I learn to rely on my spirit to dominate over my flesh, in this journey of faith?

Contemplations Response

_____

_____

_____

_____

_____

_____

_____

_____

_____

_____

Lord, what would You desire to say to me today?

_____

_____

_____

_____

_____

_____

_____

_____

_____

_____

_____

ACTIVATION PRAYER

Lord, open my eyes to see as You see, with mercy, grace, hope, and love in spite of the attitudes of others. Enable me today to "walk crushing" the enemy under my feet. Lord, I choose to break agreement with the spirit of division and come into agreement with the Holy Spirit of unity, peace and joy. Help me to see through the lens of faith, that ***"with God, all things are possible!"*** *(Matthew 19:26b)*

MY "ALONG THE WAY" STORIES

Keep this journal ready to fill in your stories when they happen!

_____

_____

_____

_____

_____

_____

_____

_____

_____

_____

_____

_____

_____

_____

_____

_____

_____

_____

_____

"He who says he abides in Him ought...to WALK JUST AS HE WALKED."
1 John 2:6

FURTHER MEDITATION: UNITY

The Lord surprised me one day, and spoke this to me:

I answered My own prayer of unity ON THE CROSS!

"For he himself is our peace, who has MADE THE TWO...ONE

and has destroyed the barrier, the dividing wall of hostility...

His purpose was to create in himself one new humanity

out of the two, thus making PEACE,

and in one body to reconcile both of them to God

through the CROSS, by which he put to death their hostility."

Ephesians 2:14-16 (NIV)

I realized my usual prayers from John 17 had been prayed amiss.
He then gave me this incredible paradigm shift:

HOW TO PRAY FOR UNITY

1. THANK ME for accomplishing UNITY on the CROSS!

2. RECEIVE this finished work by FAITH, just as we did salvation!

3. CONFESS and REPENT of your own REBELLION in HOSTILITY
   against His finished work on the cross!

4. NOW, YOU CAN STEP INTO THIS UNITY!

14

WIND AND WAVES OBEY

Matthew 8:23-27, Mark 4:35-41, Luke 8:22-25

APPLICATION

When we seek Jesus in our storms, ideally, we need to go to Him in faith! But should we go in fear, He will still respond. He is our *ever-present help in time of trouble.* (Psalm 46:10)

"Let not your heart be troubled." (John 14:1) The Lord spoke this to me one day, with an awesome challenge. ***"Trouble you will always have in this world. Keep it on the outside! Don't let it on the inside!"***

This proved to be a game-changer in my life. I know Jesus is the Prince of Peace who dwells inside of me. I like to think of it this way: I desire for Him to fill every "room" in my heart with His peace and light. If I LET trouble in, I am allowing darkness (fear, worry, frustration, stress, heaviness, etc.) to fill some rooms, displacing my Prince of Peace. I am not okay with that, so I have learned to set new boundaries against any and all troubles invading my heart. I have found that it's not as hard as it sounds. When we agree with God, He pours out His abundant grace for us to discover.

OBSERVATIONS OF THE BIBLICAL ACCOUNT

1. Preachers like to say Jesus could sleep during that time because there was **no storm** in His heart! The omnipotent One will never leave us alone in the storms of life! Fortunately, the Prince of Peace resides safely within our vessels.

2. Note the **power of words**; only three simple words by Jesus calmed the mighty waves.

COMMUNION

Open my heart, Holy Spirit, to be still and listen to Your heart. Help me to receive and believe. Prepare me for powerful new activation.

Biblical Applications and Observations

ALONG THE WAY Reflections (on the author's story)

CONTEMPLATIONS

How am I growing in understanding regarding the powerful authority from God that He has entrusted to me?

In what ways am I speaking the words of Jesus (The Word of God) over a desperate situation?

Where have I allowed trouble to invade my heart?

Contemplations Response

_____

_____

_____

_____

_____

_____

_____

_____

_____

_____

_____

Lord, what would You desire to say to me today?

_____

_____

_____

_____

_____

_____

_____

_____

_____

_____

_____

ACTIVATION PRAYER

Lord, my eyes are fixed on You; You are my great deliverer. Thank you that I can rest in Your love and your faithfulness. You are the Rock beneath my feet. Peace, be still, O my soul!

MY "ALONG THE WAY" STORIES

Keep this journal ready to fill in your stories when they happen!

"He who says he abides in Him ought...to WALK JUST AS HE WALKED."
1 John 2:6

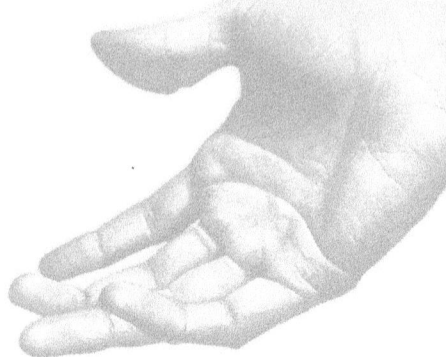

15

CASTING OUT THE LEGION

Matthew 8:28-34, Mark 5:1-20, Luke 8:26-39

APPLICATION

Though this miracle reveals how powerful the unclean spirits can be to kill 2,000 swine (unclean animals), it glorifies God so much more that the legion had to instantly obey one simple command of Jesus. We are to faint not! *We are to take our stand, like David, and boldly face whatever giants the enemy sends to intimidate us. In the name of Jesus, we are the victors!* However, amid a great victory, we must be careful to receive wisdom from above—*what next? New converts are not "ours" —they are His, to grow where He wants to plant them!*

Love must be able to both bless and release others, back into His powerful hands of grace and guidance. Just as Jesus did not sweep this man into His inner circle of followers, so are we to hold lightly to the dramatically saved, healed, or delivered —for them to serve wherever the Spirit leads. In this case, the one set free was sent to go forth right then as a light to shine in his community, where his life had so dramatically glorified the devil until now.

OBSERVATIONS OF THE BIBLICAL ACCOUNT

1. At least four of the miracles Jesus performed up to this point, involved the demonic. This one involved thousands of demons! It is interesting how prevalent they were in the "holy land!" Obviously, the enemy wanted to stake a **claim** where God's chosen people had been planted to dwell.

2. It's blatantly apparent that no one prior to Jesus seemed to know how to squelch demonic power. All the tedious religious rituals of the day had **not freed** one person from the control of those unclean spirits.

COMMUNION

Open my heart, Holy Spirit, to be still and listen to Your heart. Help me to receive and believe. Prepare me for powerful new activation.

Biblical Applications and Observations

_____

_____

_____

_____

_____

_____

_____

_____

_____

_____

ALONG THE WAY Reflections (on the author's story)

_____

_____

_____

_____

_____

_____

_____

_____

_____

CONTEMPLATIONS

How confident am I in the power of the Holy Spirit on my behalf?

How can I learn to operate in the fear of the Lord, and not the fear of the enemy?

Whose power is present within me to set the captives free?

Contemplations Response

_____

_____

_____

_____

_____

_____

_____

_____

_____

_____

_____

Lord, what would You desire to say to me today?

_____

_____

_____

_____

_____

_____

_____

_____

_____

_____

_____

ACTIVATION PRAYER

Lord, grant me keen discernment to not only set the captives free, but also to lead them back into the loving arms of Abba Father. I receive great faith, peace, power and confidence not my own, all for the glory of God! Your Kingdom come! Your will be done!

MY "ALONG THE WAY" STORIES

Keep this journal ready to fill in your stories when they happen!

"He who says he abides in Him ought...to WALK JUST AS HE WALKED."
1 John 2:6

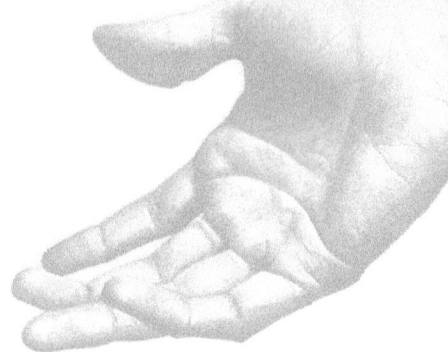

16

TWELVE-YEAR INFIRMITY

Matthew 9: 20-22, Mark 5:25-34, Luke 8:40-48

APPLICATION

This nameless woman had dared to believe, as Abraham had, for something that had never happened before! This verse came to mind: **"Against all hope, Abraham in hope believed"** for his promised son (Romans 4:18). Whereas Abraham, in fact, had a promise, this woman did not. She had nothing but her own tenacious faith and hope.

We must take this challenge to be sensitive to the Holy Spirit. We may be on an urgent prayer call to get to the hospital fast for someone in an accident, when the Holy Spirit tugs at our heart to stop on the sidewalk and turn back for a person we just passed. Or it could be the nurse who just left the room, offended by our prayer, who is the most hopeless, and needs a miracle of Love. We must not let reasoning, fear or shame hinder us.

"Humble yourselves in the sight of the Lord, and He will lift you up in honor." James 4:10 (NIV)

OBSERVATIONS OF THE BIBLICAL ACCOUNT

1. Jesus especially honors faith that is **bold** and public.

2. His bleeding heart of compassion would **not overlook one** pressing need for another.

3. **Numbers** are often a confirmation of His intentions to work: the girl who died was age **12**, the woman's infirmity had lasted **12** years. Twelve represents governing

authority. Those identical timeframes were subtle signposts of the presence of the King, taking His dominion in the land.

COMMUNION

Open my heart, Holy Spirit, to be still and listen to Your heart. Help me to receive and believe. Prepare me for powerful new activation.

Biblical Applications and Observations

_____

_____

_____

_____

_____

_____

_____

_____

_____

_____

_____

ALONG THE WAY Reflections (on the author's story)

_____

_____

_____

_____

_____

_____

_____

_____

_____

_____

_____

CONTEMPLATIONS

Where do I need to believe God to work where doctors cannot?

Without a personal promise from God in my own stormy trials, how tenacious is my faith?

When have I seen God's unique signs to indicate His timing to work?

Contemplations Response

_____

_____

_____

_____

_____

_____

_____

_____

_____

_____

Lord, what would You desire to say to me today?

_____

_____

_____

_____

_____

_____

_____

_____

_____

ACTIVATION PRAYER

Lord, enable me to soar in my expectation of Your power to bless my own life, as well as my world today. I receive ears to hear the silent cries of the needy You place in my path today.

Let my life be a power source like yours, where people KNOW they can come and be changed.

MY "ALONG THE WAY" STORIES

Keep this journal ready to fill in your stories when they happen!

_____

_____

_____

_____

_____

_____

_____

_____

_____

_____

_____

_____

_____

_____

_____

_____

_____

_____

_____

"He who says he abides in Him ought...to WALK JUST AS HE WALKED."
1 John 2:6

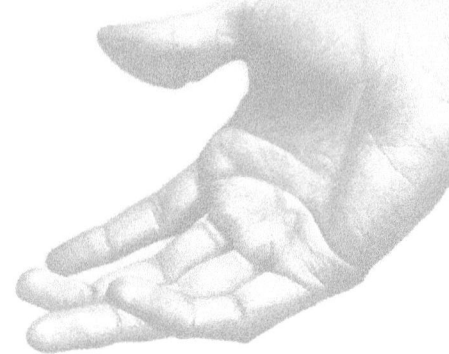

17

DAUGHTER'S RESURRECTION

Matthew 9:18-26, Mark 5:21-24, 35-43, Luke 8:40-42, 50-56

APPLICATION

We must trust God in the most trying circumstances! His delays are purposeful. His ways are higher than ours. Higher means better. We must die to our flesh when we think *we can't take it anymore* and want to give up. **"Wait on the Lord; be strong, take heart and wait for the Lord."** (Psalm 27:1) In other words, wait and keep on waiting. Waiting is not an "oops" or an oversight but is always significant. Our waiting must be a wait of faith, like Abraham's, not impatience.

Romans 4:18-20 sets a high bar for the measure of faith the Lord desires to exhibit in us:

"Against all hope, Abraham... Without weakening in his faith, he faced the fact that his body was as good as dead—since he was about 100 years old...Yet he did not waver through unbelief regarding the promise of God but was strengthened in his faith and gave glory to God, being fully persuaded that God had power to do what he had promised."

As we operate as His miracle-workers, we must listen and speak forth the bold words that we hear from the Spirit, just as Jesus did. ***"She's not dead but sleeping."*** People will laugh, but not for long. Soon they will see and celebrate with us. **"We must call things that are not before they are."** (Romans 4:17)

"The righteous are as bold as a lion" (Proverbs 28:1b)–the Lion of Judah! A good question to ask the Lord, in the case of serious illness, **"Is this a sickness unto death or life?"** (John 11:4) *Proceed accordingly!*

OBSERVATIONS OF THE BIBLICAL ACCOUNT

1. Once Jesus was allowed by the Father to minister in His supernatural power, the pleas were continuous. People were desperate and willing to look foolish in seeking help, even past the stage of death. Jesus encouraged the father of the dead girl to grow his **faith** in the face of death.

2. It's **never too late**. Despite the mixture of faith and fear that He saw in this seeker, Love responded freely to the miracle request.

"Wait on the Lord;
BE STRONG,
take heart and wait for the Lord."
Psalm 27:1

COMMUNION

Open my heart, Holy Spirit, to be still and listen to Your heart. Help me to receive and believe. Prepare me for powerful new activation.

Biblical Applications and Observations

_____

_____

_____

_____

_____

_____

_____

_____

_____

_____

_____

_____

_____

ALONG THE WAY Reflections (on the author's story)

_____

_____

_____

_____

_____

_____

_____

_____

_____

_____

CONTEMPLATIONS

How can I learn to press past my fears, into the place of great faith?

Am I trusting the Lord with faith and hope to override a doctor's bleak report?

How can I better prepare to walk in His resurrection power?

Contemplations Response

Lord, what would You desire to say to me today?

ACTIVATION PRAYER

Lord, empower me to open my mouth wide with the boldness of a lion to silence the enemy. Open my eyes to see clearly the arm of the Lord ready to release Life into any death camps I must face. Use my life daily to glorify the Giver of Life!

MY "ALONG THE WAY" STORIES

Keep this journal ready to fill in your stories when they happen!

_____

_____

_____

_____

_____

_____

_____

_____

_____

_____

_____

_____

_____

_____

_____

_____

_____

_____

_____

_____

"He who says he abides in Him ought...to WALK JUST AS HE WALKED."
1 John 2:6

Abraham set a HIGH BAR for the measure
of faith

that the Lord desires to exhibit in us.

"Against all hope, Abraham…
Without weakening in his faith,
he faced the fact that his body was as good as
dead—since he was about 100 years old…

Yet he did NOT WAVER through unbelief
regarding the promise of God
but was STRENGTHENED in his faith
and gave glory to God,
being fully persuaded that God had power
to do what He had promised."
Romans 4:18-20 NIV

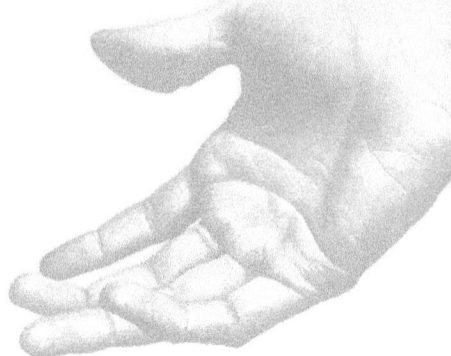

18

RESTORING SIGHT TO THE BLIND

Matthew 9:27-31

APPLICATION

Then He touched their eyes and said, "According to your faith let it be to you." (Matthew 9:29) That same Voice of power and authority has been entrusted to us, in the Name of Jesus. The Light of the world dwells within us—the Voice of the Light, the Creator of all Life, the Resurrection and the Life.

"Is anything too difficult for the Lord?" (Genesis 18:14, Jeremiah 32:17, 27) Is anything too difficult for the Lord *in me*? No.

It is only my difficulty in believing and yielding to this all powerful One dwelling within, that hinders me. His challenge to me is to shut the door to doubt! ***"Out with doubt,"*** He once instructed me. Instead, I am to choose great and growing faith—to believe, obey, open my mouth, speak Light, speak truth in love, and let Him change the world through me.

Yes, Lord! Have your way! Four of the most powerful words we can learn to release are those first miraculous words: **"Let there be light!"** (Genesis 1:3) Darkness must flee!

OBSERVATIONS OF THE BIBLICAL ACCOUNT

1. A vital key in my daily journey of faith is to keep saying, ***Yes, Lord!*** Those two powerful words open the door to His presence and His power being manifested in amazing ways, both to me and through me.

2. Answers come according to the measure of my **faith.**

COMMUNION

Open my heart, Holy Spirit, to be still and listen to Your heart. Help me to receive and believe. Prepare me for powerful new activation.

Biblical Applications and Observations

_____

_____

_____

_____

_____

_____

_____

_____

_____

_____

_____

ALONG THE WAY Reflections (on the author's story)

_____

_____

_____

_____

_____

_____

_____

_____

_____

_____

_____

_____

CONTEMPLATIONS

How can I give the Lord my "YES" in all things?
Have I given up on an old prayer request?
How can I learn to see with my heart what I cannot see with my eyes?

Contemplations Response

Lord, what would You desire to say to me today?

ACTIVATION PRAYER

Lord, open my eyes and ears to see and to hear what I have been missing. Open my mouth also to be the voice of mercy and light for others, to obliterate encroaching darkness. I repent of any old agreements with darkness and choose to only agree with the voice of truth and light!

MY "ALONG THE WAY" STORIES

Keep this journal ready to fill in your stories when they happen!

"He who says he abides in Him ought...to WALK JUST AS HE WALKED."
1 John 2:6

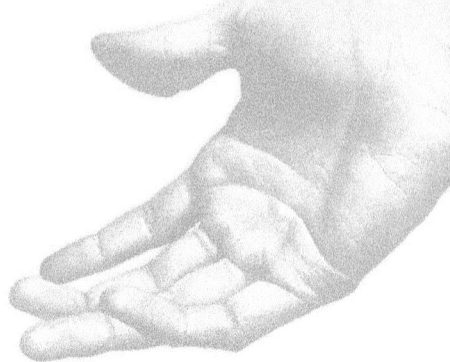

19

THE MUTE SPEAKS

Matthew 9:32-34

APPLICATION

Ministry in the name of the Lord is awesome, yet trying, demanding and likely to be judged and misunderstood. Who are we to please? Only One—no one else, not even ourselves. And so, we press on—**"for the joy set before us."** (Hebrews 12:2) We must endure any onslaught of attack. One day, His words will reward our obedience, despite all the trials: **"Well done, good and faithful servant!"** (Matthew 25:23)

We must not limit ourselves to one success story at a time. Perhaps there will be a whole roomful. We must keep going, as the Spirit leads. We don't want our success in the morning to rob us of more success in the afternoon.

OBSERVATIONS OF THE BIBLICAL ACCOUNT

1. Though Jesus knew His power would free the man and bring further ridicule upon Himself, He pressed on in His compassion that was **"new every morning!"** (Lamentations 3:23) His compass was clearly set to demonstrate **loving others** ahead of His own comfort, in eager obedience to the Father's heart.

2. At the same time, the **voice of the enemy** was growing louder in his hatred, fear, and jealousy of the Messiah, as the voice of darkness overruled any compassion the Pharisees may have had.

COMMUNION

Open my heart, Holy Spirit, to be still and listen to Your heart. Help me to receive and believe. Prepare me for powerful new activation.

Biblical Applications and Observations

_____

_____

_____

_____

_____

_____

_____

_____

_____

_____

_____

_____

ALONG THE WAY Reflections (on the author's story)

_____

_____

_____

_____

_____

_____

_____

_____

_____

_____

_____

_____

CONTEMPLATIONS

"Is anything too hard for the Lord?" (Genesis 18:14)

Do I have a stronghold of shyness* that blocks me from being myself? If so, how can love and concern for others help me break this stronghold?

How can I cooperate with the Lord for a breakthrough of NEW boldness in my life?

NOTE: This is usually rooted in <u>fear and pride</u> because of a self-focus. Choose a new mindset of thinking of others more than self. Confess and repent of both. Thank Him for grace to walk in new freedom.

Contemplations Response

_____

_____

_____

_____

_____

_____

_____

_____

_____

_____

Lord, what would You desire to say to me today?

_____

_____

_____

_____

_____

_____

_____

_____

_____

ACTIVATION PRAYER

*Lord, help me to move past the stage of agony into the stage of full surrender and power, laying down my life (comfort, convenience, will, time) for my brothers and sisters daily. Use me to speak bold words of life and healing in hopeless situations. Thank You, Lord, that You are ready to do a **"new thing,"** (see Isaiah 43:19) in me and through me for others!*

*I say, **"YES LORD!"***

MY "ALONG THE WAY" STORIES

Keep this journal ready to fill in your stories when they happen!

_____

_____

_____

_____

_____

_____

_____

_____

_____

_____

_____

_____

_____

_____

_____

_____

_____

_____

"He who says he abides in Him ought...to WALK JUST AS HE WALKED."
1 John 2:6

20

POOL OF BETHESDA ON THE SABBATH

John 5:1-21, 30

APPLICATION

We are the ones He is compelling to take the hurting ones by the hand and show them how easy it is to step into His healing pool. ***Come!***

The waters have been stirring since the days of Jesus.

Today is the day. The masses are awaiting the faith and love coursing from our hearts.

OBSERVATIONS OF THE BIBLICAL ACCOUNT

1. The man by the pool persisted but had likely become quite hopeless in his waiting. Jesus always required a **spoken request** of the need—an expression of faith. Finally, after 38 years, the man received his "suddenly" blessing!

2. The Lord spoke forth the clearest insight yet as to how the **healing process** worked. "Jesus gave them this answer, '**Very truly** [Greek: **Amen, amen,**] **I tell you, the Son can do nothing by himself; He can do only what He sees His Father doing, because whatever the Father does the Son also does.**'" (John 5:19)

*(NOTE: Jesus was the first person in the Bible to use **"amen" at the beginning** of a thought; scholars believe He used it to emphasize and confirm what He was about to say. It seems unfortunate that translators decided to change His word in translation. Jesus likes to be creative, and He certainly has a very intentional way with words.)*

COMMUNION

Open my heart, Holy Spirit, to be still and listen to Your heart. Help me to receive and believe. Prepare me for powerful new activation.

Biblical Applications and Observations

_____

_____

_____

_____

_____

_____

_____

_____

_____

_____

_____

ALONG THE WAY Reflections (on the author's story)

_____

_____

_____

_____

_____

_____

_____

_____

_____

_____

_____

CONTEMPLATIONS

How should I think and pray differently to become more flexible with my time?
How do I see my heart being softened for the needs of others?
When has my compassion risen up to weep for the hurting ones?

Contemplations Response

Lord, what would You desire to say to me today?

ACTIVATION PRAYER

Lord, I am ready to celebrate the new life to be released through my prayers! Thank you that Your healing hand will connect my heart to those who are ready to receive their blessing. As I sow in tears, thank You I will be reaping in joy! Let others see You in me now—the Blesser. Thank you, Lord, for arriving on the scene before me every time!

MY "ALONG THE WAY" STORIES

Keep this journal ready to fill in your stories when they happen!

"He who says he abides in Him ought...to WALK JUST AS HE WALKED."
1 John 2:6

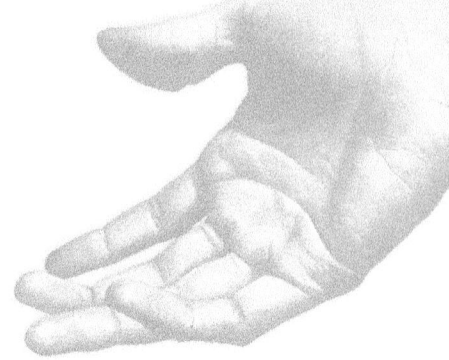

21

MIRACLE OF IMPARTATION TO THE TWELVE

Matthew 10:1-41, Mark 6:7-13, Luke 9:1-6

APPLICATION

We must receive Jesus' unlimited power and anointing to magnify Him today. The NIV states, **"As you go, proclaim this message: 'The kingdom of heaven has come near.' Heal the sick, raise the dead."** When I looked up the **Greek** in *Scripture4All* for Matthew 10:7, I felt more encouraged than ever as I read the actual verbs written:

"GOING yet BE PROCLAIMING

saying that the kingdom of heaven has neared,

be CURING the infirmed...dead ones BE ROUSING!"

How powerfully it is all stated with *continuous* action. The Holy Spirit immediately planted this in my mind: **Going! Proclaiming! Curing! Rousing!!** This became my new "along the way" *modus operandum!* How incredible that we are truly empowered like this!

Let's continue to say, "Yes, Lord!" to His powerful plan!

ALL of us as believers are the called ones and the sent ones.

Next, we must realize, as we begin to see success, that this is not *my* special ministry. It is simply my yielding fully to His power. As I pray over others, I must also bless them to begin walking in the same healing anointing. I am to help awaken others to this process of yielding to Him, to multiply the sent ones upon the earth!

Going! Proclaiming! Curing! Rousing!

OBSERVATIONS OF THE BIBLICAL ACCOUNT

1. These twelve would still have been fairly new disciples at the time! It had likely been only a few months since they had responded to His invitation to **"Follow Me."** Now the Lord had altered the call, to **"go forth,"** two by two.

2. Three times He instructed them to **"fear not!"**

Mark 16:20 conveys the Lord's great plan
to work among all His obedient servants
who will work for the great harvest:
"Then the disciples went out and preached everywhere,
and the LORD WORKED WITH THEM
and confirmed His word by the SIGNS
that accompanied it."

COMMUNION

Open my heart, Holy Spirit, to be still and listen to Your heart. Help me to receive and believe. Prepare me for powerful new activation.

Biblical Applications and Observations

ALONG THE WAY Reflections (on the author's story)

CONTEMPLATIONS

Have I ever thought to receive my impartation of power from the Lord, as His follower?
How could I gain a new mindset of: going, proclaiming, curing, and rousing?
Who could I "go forth" with to practice releasing His healing power and love?

Contemplations Response

_____

_____

_____

_____

_____

_____

_____

_____

_____

_____

Lord, what would You desire to say to me today?

_____

_____

_____

_____

_____

_____

_____

_____

_____

_____

ACTIVATION PRAYER

*O Lord, grant me ears to hear, as You lead me to **go forth** and also to empower others. Thank You, Lord, for my great joy and delight in my service to the King! Here I am! Use me! Freely I have received; freely I will give! Thank you for imparting your power and authority upon me, in Your great and mighty name.*

MY "ALONG THE WAY" STORIES

Keep this journal ready to fill in your stories when they happen!

_____

_____

_____

_____

_____

_____

"He who says he abides in Him ought...to WALK JUST AS HE WALKED."
1 John 2:6

Thank you, Lord,
for Your **powerful impartation** even today!

This coincides with this wisdom He gave me once:

The 3 A's

Alignment + Activation = Acceleration

Alignment = to agree with Him/His word, and not doubt
Activation = to be obedient to act on our faith
Acceleration = the results will now happen more quickly!

Without proper alignment, nothing will happen!

22

FEEDING THE MULTITUDE: 5000 MEN

Matthew 14:14-21, Mark 6:31-44, Luke 9:10-17, John 6:5-13

APPLICATION

Our thoughts must grow to stay elevated up above the natural. We are to ignore the "CAN'T" mindset and celebrate the fact *that* we **"can do all things through Christ who strengthens us."** (Philippians 4:13) In the Greek (*Scripture4All.com*) it reads. "In all I am being strong in One 'abling' me"...

We are *best* qualified to serve Him and operate in the glory realm by our *inadequacies*. He chooses us especially because of those inadequacies. Our *need* is to draw us squarely before Him in expectation and readiness to tell the world of His faithfulness, both before and after the results transpire! His power and strength qualify us. We walk by faith, we speak by faith, we run by faith, and we finish by faith.

Let's look to see where our loaves and fishes are waiting for His blessing.

OBSERVATIONS OF THE BIBLICAL ACCOUNT

1. The account simply states there had been 5,000 men, so the total meals He provided, including women and children had to be **well over 10,000!**

2. Jesus' love and compassion for mankind was **not depleted**, despite the deep sorrow over His cousin's tragic execution. There was basically no time for Him to mourn.

3. This is the **only miracle** that is told in all four gospels, prior to Jesus' arrest.

COMMUNION

Open my heart, Holy Spirit, to be still and listen to Your heart. Help me to receive and believe. Prepare me for powerful new activation.

Biblical Applications and Observations

_____
_____
_____
_____
_____
_____
_____
_____
_____
_____
_____
_____
_____

ALONG THE WAY Reflections (on the author's story)

_____
_____
_____
_____
_____
_____
_____
_____
_____
_____
_____
_____

CONTEMPLATIONS

How do my limitations limit Him?

How often do I wake up with great expectations in my heart for the day?

How do I need to let Him shift my mindset for life without limits?

Contemplations Response

_____

_____

_____

_____

_____

_____

_____

_____

_____

_____

Lord, what would You desire to say to me today?

_____

_____

_____

_____

_____

_____

_____

_____

_____

_____

_____

ACTIVATION PRAYER

Lord, today I am choosing to align with new expectancy in this Kingdom business I am in! I also choose to speak words of LIFE in the face of death! Fill my heart with faith overflowing for the impossible. Use my voice to resound with hope when others are speaking fear and despair.

MY "ALONG THE WAY" STORIES

Keep this journal ready to fill in your stories when they happen!

"He who says he abides in Him ought...to WALK JUST AS HE WALKED."
1 John 2:6

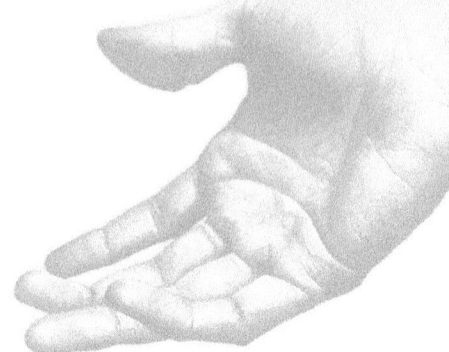

23

PETER WALKS ON THE WATER

Matthew 14:22-33 (Mark 6:45-52, John 6:16-23)

APPLICATION

We need ears to hear His "*COME!*" When others say, "impossible," let me be quick to say, "possible!"

His thoughts, His ways are higher than ours. Let's give freedom to the **"mind of Christ"** (I Corinthians 2:16) to operate in us. We must graduate out of the mundane, the natural, to dwell in the supernatural realm, in thoughts, words, and deeds.

"As he thinks in his heart, so is he." (Proverbs 23:7)

We must learn to cancel all thoughts that do not exhibit the supernatural ways of our Lord, the Anointed One. May we learn to walk continuously in the same bold, awe-filled, faith-filled power and anointing as our Lord, who happens to be resident inside us. The Lord never said that someone's faith was too BIG! *Increase our faith, Lord!*

OBSERVATIONS OF THE BIBLICAL ACCOUNT

1. *Strangely, only Matthew related this account of Peter walking on the water!* Mark and John told the rest of the story, omitting **Peter's bold** actions. Did they regret not stepping out themselves? (Since all Scripture is inspired, however; we have no explanation about that.)

2. Mark focused on another unique point: **"They were greatly amazed, for they had not understood about the loaves; their hearts were hardened."** (Mark 6:51-52 NIV)

COMMUNION

Open my heart, Holy Spirit, to be still and listen to Your heart. Help me to receive and believe. Prepare me for powerful new activation.

Biblical Applications and Observations

_____
_____
_____
_____
_____
_____
_____
_____
_____
_____
_____
_____
_____

ALONG THE WAY Reflections (on the author's story)

_____
_____
_____
_____
_____
_____
_____
_____
_____
_____
_____
_____
_____

CONTEMPLATIONS

Is my boldness and faith resilient despite the attitudes of others?
Where do I dwell amidst a storm, in peace or turmoil? Why?
Would the Lord look at me and say I have great faith?

Contemplations Response

Lord, what would You desire to say to me today?

ACTIVATION PRAYER

Lord, enable me to keep my eyes on You, in the darkest times and to live in great expectancy for Your power to flow through me. Vanquish all waves of fear that would attempt to hinder the supernatural being released in my life. I'm choosing to keep my eyes on You, and desire to be called "fearless" in my faith and obedience.

MY "ALONG THE WAY" STORIES

Keep this journal ready to fill in your stories when they happen!

"He who says he abides in Him ought...to WALK JUST AS HE WALKED."
1 John 2:6

24

MULTITUDES HEALED IN GENNESARET

Matthew 14:34-36, Mark 6:53-56

APPLICATION

At home, in the marketplace, at school, at the gas stations, all along the way, everyday life must be transferred into the powerful realm of the Kingdom. The blessing of the life-flow of the Lord must become the life-flow of our heartbeat. We must see the individual, as well as the masses and seek to save them, heal them, and deliver them in Jesus' Name.

We must SO love our world!

Flesh must die for our Spirits to soar in His Kingdom power of sacrificial love, compassion and grace.

OBSERVATIONS OF THE BIBLICAL ACCOUNT

1. The healing of the woman's flow of blood (see Chapter 16) had evidently made a lasting impression with her onlookers, as her words, **"if I could only touch the hem of your garment,"** had been quoted here by others. Her gutsy humility had birthed her greatness.

2. In Matthew 14:35, **"People brought all their sick to him."** It is interesting to note that the Greek for sick or ill is *kakos,* which also means evil. This provides an inference to the source of the sickness! This is confirmed when we consider John 10:10, **"the thief** (devil) **comes to rob, kill, destroy, but I** (Jesus) **have come to give life and life more abundantly."**

COMMUNION

Open my heart, Holy Spirit, to be still and listen to Your heart. Help me to receive and believe. Prepare me for powerful new activation.

Biblical Applications and Observations

_____

_____

_____

_____

_____

_____

_____

_____

_____

_____

_____

_____

_____

ALONG THE WAY Reflections (on the author's story)

_____

_____

_____

_____

_____

_____

_____

_____

_____

_____

_____

_____

CONTEMPLATIONS

How can I more readily value healings of the heart?

Why do I still struggle to believe that I can be His powerful arm of healing?

How does the marketplace see the love of Jesus when I walk through?

Contemplations Response

_____

_____

_____

_____

_____

_____

_____

_____

_____

_____

Lord, what would You desire to say to me today?

_____

_____

_____

_____

_____

_____

_____

_____

_____

_____

_____

_____

ACTIVATION PRAYER

Bless me with bold, vibrant prayers that shock even myself. Enable me to lay down my life and my time, to 'so love' the world. May my love and tenacity for breakthrough be the proof of Your soaring freedom in my life.

MY "ALONG THE WAY" STORIES

Keep this journal ready to fill in your stories when they happen!

"He who says he abides in Him ought...to WALK JUST AS HE WALKED."
1 John 2:6

25

DAUGHTER OF A GENTILE WOMAN

Matthew 15:21-28, Mark 7:31-37

APPLICATION

Who do we categorize as unworthy or unreachable?

Occultic? Murderers? Terrorists?

None is beyond the payment of the blood of Jesus, already provided in full. It is our place to extend the Lord's invitation to all.

"Come! All who are thirsty. . ." (Isaiah 55:1)

Come pick up His gift for you! It is as if the Lord has left free tickets for the whole world at the "Will Call" station—His love, mercy, grace, salvation, power, and purpose.

As we go forth, we cannot disqualify anyone around us. According to the testimonies of many who offer prayer on the streets, it seems there are more miracles happening for the unbeliever (such as Muslims or atheists) than for the believer. God is fervently choosing to reveal His heart of love to the lost and desperate through His powerful healings. In some places, whole people groups are turning to God as Savior through just one miracle.

"For He himself is our peace, who has made the two groups one and has destroyed the barrier, the dividing wall of hostility. . . and in one body to reconcile both of them to God through the cross, by which he put to death their hostility."
(Ephesians 2:14, 16 NIV)

OBSERVATIONS OF THE BIBLICAL ACCOUNT

1. Whereas Jesus had His privacy for thirty years, once His public ministry began, He could scarcely find time to be alone. **Hunger** for the supernatural seemed rampant since it had been 400 years since God had spoken upon the earth.

2. The words Jesus spoke to the woman in this account have always been extremely disturbing. His words sound uncaring and **harsh** to us, over 2,000 years later. But this appears to be a pivotal moment for Jesus, who *only did what He saw the Father do, and said what He heard the Father say.*

3. Until now, **grace** had not been extended beyond the Israelite people whom He had been sent to serve. Full unmerited grace to the Gentiles would only later be released after the cross, when He shed His blood for all.

The Pharisees considered themselves "clean"
and would not call Him Lord;
they considered her "unclean"
and yet she called Him Lord.

COMMUNION

Open my heart, Holy Spirit, to be still and listen to Your heart. Help me to receive and believe. Prepare me for powerful new activation.

Biblical Applications and Observations

_____

_____

_____

_____

_____

_____

_____

_____

_____

_____

_____

_____

ALONG THE WAY Reflections (on the author's story)

_____

_____

_____

_____

_____

_____

_____

_____

_____

_____

_____

_____

_____

CONTEMPLATIONS

Who do I categorize as unworthy or unreachable?

Where does the Lord want me to begin sowing seeds of grace in the hard ground around me?

What have I done that I may consider to be unforgivable? Am I ready to forgive myself?

Contemplations Response

Lord, what would You desire to say to me today?

ACTIVATION PRAYER

Fill my heart Lord, with Yours. Minister Your love freely through these hands. Transcend all barriers and walls that You see in my heart. May Your love implode and explode in and out of this vessel, for all the world to see!

MY "ALONG THE WAY" STORIES

Keep this journal ready to fill in your stories when they happen!

"He who says he abides in Him ought...to WALK JUST AS HE WALKED."
1 John 2:6

The woman came and knelt before Him,
"LORD, HELP ME!"
He replied,
**"It is not right to take the children's bread and
toss it to the dogs."**

"Yes it is, Lord," she said. "Even the dogs eat the
crumbs
that fall from their master's table."

Then He told her,
**"Woman, you have great faith!
Your request is granted.
For such a reply, you may go;
the demon has left your daughter."**
Matthew 15: 25-28, Mark 7:29 NIV

"Humble yourselves before the Lord and
He will lift you up."
James 4:10 NIV

26

HEALING OF A DEAF MAN

Mark 7:31-36

APPLICATION

Do we have ears to hear the Spirit and a heart to obey in hard places of obedience? From the perspective of becoming His hands of healing—would we be willing to do the odd thing (as Jesus spat on the ground) that He may have shown us in our mind's eye, as a prophetic act in the healing? Obviously, Jesus could have simply spoken the healing words. But the Father had him spit and then touch the man's tongue. The man wasn't blind, so he was probably shocked and repulsed. *But he was also healed.*

Lord, be Lord! The Father has His wise ways of testing us, even during ministry. Will we do it His way or ours? Since we know our way doesn't work, and His does, whatever He desires, we must be prepared to do. *We need to decide ahead of time that to look foolish in our obedience will be fine!* It's another moment for our flesh to die and our spirit to soar, in full obedience. Kingdom power flows in such places of difficult obedience. When God does something amazing for us, is it now *our* story to tell whenever and wherever we want? No, rather it is still His work, to honor Him and wait for His wisdom and guidance, regarding when to share it!

OBSERVATIONS OF THE BIBLICAL ACCOUNT

1. Perhaps when He knew that He was to spit and touch the man's tongue, He felt He should withdraw from the crowd. Yet, He only did what He saw the **Father** do.

2. Our challenge continually is to not **"lean not on our own understanding,"** as in Proverbs 3:5a.

COMMUNION

Open my heart, Holy Spirit, to be still and listen to Your heart. Help me to receive and believe. Prepare me for powerful new activation.

Biblical Applications and Observations

ALONG THE WAY Reflections (on the author's story)

CONTEMPLATIONS

What are my burning questions for the Lord today?

When have I trusted the wisdom of the Lord that made no sense?

How am I developing my *ears to hear* the Holy Spirit?

Contemplations Response

_____

_____

_____

_____

_____

_____

_____

_____

_____

_____

_____

Lord, what would You desire to say to me today?

_____

_____

_____

_____

_____

_____

_____

_____

_____

_____

ACTIVATION PRAYER

Holy Spirit, I choose to surrender now in preparation for going forth in careful obedience to Your leading. Thank You for calling me to be a miracle-worker in the Name of Jesus, to heal the one in front of me, and the masses, as You lead and direct me. I lay my ways on the altar, and choose only Your ways, O Lord.

MY "ALONG THE WAY" STORIES

Keep this journal ready to fill in your stories when they happen!

"He who says he abides in Him ought...to WALK JUST AS HE WALKED."
1 John 2:6

27

HEALING AND FEEDING A MULTITUDE AGAIN

Matthew 15:29-39, Mark 8:1-10

APPLICATION

How the Lord loves to answer this prayer: *Increase my hunger, Lord!*

I first prayed about that for myself twenty years prior to this study. That hunger has never left! Just now, in writing this, the realization has come that when He speaks to us today, His Bread within us continues to be multiplied! As we take and eat, we are to be filled full to overflowing, to turn and offer our world the best Bread of Life.

"Blessed are those who hunger and thirst for righteousness for they shall be filled." (Matthew 5:6 NIV)

He gives us multiplied basketfuls to share! Let's DO IT and do so generously.

OBSERVATIONS OF THE BIBLICAL ACCOUNT

1. This was the first mention of the **maimed** made whole. [Greek: *cured, healed*] By now, however, the supernatural had become *expected* in the ongoing journey of the disciples as they followed Jesus.

2. They had no doubt gained a **greater measure** of faith since the last time He had asked them how many loaves they had, having seen bread and fish multiply only a few days before.

COMMUNION

Open my heart, Holy Spirit, to be still and listen to Your heart. Help me to receive and believe. Prepare me for powerful new activation.

Biblical Applications and Observations

ALONG THE WAY Reflections (on the author's story)

CONTEMPLATIONS

What evidence do I see that my faith is growing?

How expectant am I to see what I have never seen before?

Do I value receiving His spiritual manna as highly as my physical intake of food today?

Contemplations Response

_____

_____

_____

_____

_____

_____

_____

_____

_____

_____

_____

Lord, what would You desire to say to me today?

_____

_____

_____

_____

_____

_____

_____

_____

_____

_____

_____

_____

ACTIVATION PRAYER

Lord, increase my hunger to pursue the Bread of Life daily. Fill me that I may then bless a needy world around me. Use me to feed those around me who are hungry.

MY "ALONG THE WAY" STORIES

Keep this journal ready to fill in your stories when they happen!

"He who says he abides in Him ought...to WALK JUST AS HE WALKED."
1 John 2:6

28

BLIND MAN HEALED AT BETHSAIDA

Mark 8:22-26

APPLICATION

We must align the beat of our hearts to the Lord's, to see the wounded hearts that He sees. Walking in the Spirit, He will release that for us, deep unto deep. As Love consumes us, Wisdom and discernment will arise and instruct us.

We will know what action we must take. His sufficiency wants to grace us now as we meditate and observe His ways. We must obey.

In my own prayers for boldness in praying healing for strangers, the Lord once gave me some simple advice: ***"Whenever I give you a nudge towards a person to offer prayer, don't debate!"***

You'll know. *Don't debate.*

OBSERVATIONS OF THE BIBLICAL ACCOUNT

1. Both times that He was led to use saliva, He took the person away from the crowd, apparently **not to humiliate** the person or to spark undue criticism. (See chapter 24.)

2. This is the only account where He led someone **by the hand** as they walked. It is also the only time we are told He prayed twice for the same healing. It seems to be purposeful to encourage us to not give up when the instantaneous miracle does not happen.

COMMUNION

Open my heart, Holy Spirit, to be still and listen to Your heart. Help me to receive and believe. Prepare me for powerful new activation.

Biblical Applications and Observations

ALONG THE WAY Reflections (on the author's story)

CONTEMPLATIONS

Have I put my hand in His hand to receive His unique flow of love that I need?
Can I choose now to agree with the Lord the next time I want to disagree?
When others say *impossible,* will I say *possible*?

Contemplations Response

_____

_____

_____

_____

_____

_____

_____

_____

_____

_____

_____

_____

Lord, what would You desire to say to me today?

_____

_____

_____

_____

_____

_____

_____

_____

_____

_____

ACTIVATION PRAYER

*Lord, help me to gain a reputation far and wide as a **bold one**, who does not shrink back. Allow me the faith to zealously pursue the works of darkness with your penetrating light of faith, hope, and love. Use me to open blind eyes!*

MY "ALONG THE WAY" STORIES

Keep this journal ready to fill in your stories when they happen!

"He who says he abides in Him ought...to WALK JUST AS HE WALKED."
1 John 2:6

29

BOY WITH EPILEPSY

Mathew 17:14-21, Mark 9:14-29, Luke 9:37-42

APPLICATION

A few days after I heard the revelation shared in this chapter, the Lord spoke to me further about my own preparation to walk in His authority.

He simply said, *"Daily fasting."*

I knew He meant for a long time, perhaps a lifetime. He impressed me that I could choose various ways to fast, and in this way, I would become more amply prepared for whatever He would allow me to confront unexpectedly along the way. My response would not be from simply an obedient obligation to His call, but with greater compassion and sensitivity to His Spirit.

He saw my desperate heart in this pursuit and was answering my cry for help to be His hands and feet. *And He said to them all,* **"If any man will come after me, let him deny himself, and take up his cross daily, and follow Me."** (Luke 9:24)

However severe the challenges before us, He will make a way for us to see the breakthrough, as we keep our eyes on Him and choose to 'love our neighbor', every day and everywhere.

OBSERVATIONS OF THE BIBLICAL ACCOUNT

1. This man was **desperate** enough to be heard, calling out from the multitude!

2. Jesus let us know His patience was being tested by the entire generation. What would He say to *our* generation, to the houses of worship where we convene, or to

my own family? Would He echo those words, **"How long shall I put up with you?"** (Mark 9:19 NIV)

3. The power and authority of our God was starkly demonstrated—a lifetime of demonic torment ended as Jesus spoke only one **brief command**. The demon had no option but to obey Him! The child was free and finally at peace.

Then the disciples came to Jesus privately and said,
"Why could we not cast it out?"
Jesus said to them,
"Because of your unbelief. . .However,
*this kind does not go out except by **prayer and fasting.**"*
Matthew 17:19-21

COMMUNION

Open my heart, Holy Spirit, to be still and listen to Your heart. Help me to receive and believe. Prepare me for powerful new activation.

Biblical Applications and Observations

_____

_____

_____

_____

_____

_____

_____

_____

_____

_____

_____

_____

_____

ALONG THE WAY Reflections (on the author's story)

_____

_____

_____

_____

_____

_____

_____

_____

_____

_____

_____

_____

CONTEMPLATIONS

Am I learning to practice various fasts as He leads?

How well have I overcome my spiritual battles with the enemy?

Am I willing to intervene to help others despite any feelings of inadequacy?

Contemplations Response

Lord, what would You desire to say to me today?

ACTIVATION PRAYER

Grow my heart Lord, to fast and pray as You lead, to be more fully prepared. Prepare me to speak LIFE into the most unlikely places as Your powerful mouthpiece for peace and restoration! Have your way, O Lord. Thank you for the victory!

MY "ALONG THE WAY" STORIES

Keep this journal ready to fill in your stories when they happen!

"He who says he abides in Him ought...to WALK JUST AS HE WALKED."
1 John 2:6

FURTHER MEDITATION: FASTING

Different types of fasts are listed here. Let the Holy Spirit lead you.

A.   There are complete water fasts.

B.   There are "Daniel fasts," taken from the diet of Daniel, which was only vegetables. (See Daniel 1:12-16)

C.   There are other partial fasts, such as only fasting during the daylight hours.

D.   The Holy Spirit may give you specific instructions to fast from something specific for an extended time, such as "sweets until I tell you." *He said this to me once, and it lasted six months. However, He took away my desire for sweets the second day!*

By far, the KEY passage on fasting to glean from is the entire chapter of **Isaiah 58.**

"Is that what you call a fast, a day acceptable to the LORD?

'Is not this the kind of fasting I have chosen:

to <u>loose </u>the chains of injustice and <u>untie</u> the cords of the yoke,

to <u>set the oppressed free</u> and <u>break</u> every yoke?

Is it not to share your food with the hungry and to provide the poor wanderer with shelter, when you see the naked, to clothe him, and not to turn away from your own flesh and blood? Then your light will break forth like the dawn, and your healing will quickly appear; then your righteousness will go before you, and the glory of the LORD will be your rear guard. Then you will call, and the LORD will answer; you will cry for help, and he will say: Here am I.' " (Isaiah 58:5-9)

Apparently, fasting is not just to "get something" or to move in greater power. It is to make heart changes in us. It is also to fight against all types of oppression, not just physical healing.

For deeper insight and motivation for the complete water fast**, I highly recommend a book** that helped spark a **worldwide movement of revival and miracles** in 1946-47. *ATOMIC POWER with God Thru Fasting and Prayer*, by Franklin Hall (1946).

(Although this book is now out of print, used copies are still available for purchase online.)

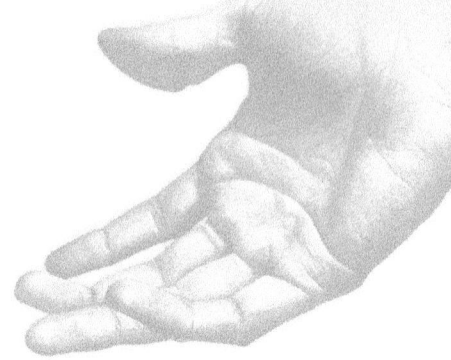

30

GO FISH FOR A COIN

Matthew 17:24-27

APPLICATION

Expect the unexpected. Never doubt He is able!
Be obedient. Run the great race of faith!

Go catch your special fish.

What may appear to be a small fish may prove to be the most valuable one in the lake.

Borrowing Mary's words here, **"Whatever He tells you, do it!"** (John 2:5)

Then get ready to be amazed!

"Ask and it will be given to you; seek, and you will find; knock, and it will be opened to you." (Matthew 7:7)

OBSERVATIONS OF THE BIBLICAL ACCOUNT

1. The Lord took this financial issue of taxes and used it as a teaching moment for salvation. In our **adoption** as children, through the redemption of His blood for our sins, our salvation is freely provided. Only the unsaved will have to pay for their sins one day.

2. Though we are not told the rest of the story, obviously the instructions He gave would have unfolded just as He said. The Lord took care of his own tax and Peter's in this miraculous provision. In all things, life with Jesus meant seeing everything saturated in the **supernatural**!

COMMUNION

Open my heart, Holy Spirit, to be still and listen to Your heart. Help me to receive and believe. Prepare me for powerful new activation.

Biblical Applications and Observations

ALONG THE WAY Reflections (on the author's story)

CONTEMPLATIONS

What is my latest testimony of God as my "ever-present-help?"
Do I view certain things as too insignificant to bother praying about?
Am I missing God's intricate involvement in my everyday life?

Contemplations Response

_____
_____
_____
_____
_____
_____
_____
_____
_____
_____
_____
_____

Lord, what would You desire to say to me today?

_____
_____
_____
_____
_____
_____
_____
_____
_____
_____

ACTIVATION PRAYER

O *Lord, when insurmountable problems interrupt my day, may I rise up with uncanny confidence to seek and to soar in Your supernatural ways! I am thanking you ahead of time for the coins You have planted in my fish. Keep me seeking Your face and pressing in for more of Your supernatural ways.*

MY "ALONG THE WAY" STORIES

Keep this journal ready to fill in your stories when they happen!

_____

_____

_____

_____

_____

_____

_____

_____

_____

_____

_____

_____

_____

_____

_____

_____

_____

_____

_____

_____

"He who says he abides in Him ought...to WALK JUST AS HE WALKED."
1 John 2:6

NOTATIONS:
THE FIRST 30 MIRACLES

Miracles recorded by book:

Matthew **22**

Mark **20**

Luke **18**

John **4**

John mostly shared the teachings of the Lord.

However, three of the miracles that John *does* record are not even told in the other three gospels.

They are:

Chapter 1. Water to Wine at the Wedding (John 2:1-11)

Chapter 12. Nobleman's Son Restored (John 4:46-54)

Chapter 20. Pool of Bethesda on the Sabbath (John 5:1-21, 30)

Only one miracle in chapters 1 through 30 is in all 4 gospels:

Chapter 22. Feeding the Multitude of 5,000 Men

(Matthew 14:14-21, Mark 6:31-44, Luke 9:10-17, John 6:5-13)

Whereas,

many people recommend young believers begin reading the Bible with *The Gospel of John*, very few miracles would be included.

I am questioning that reasoning now, because to new believers, it seems the testimonies of His many miracles would be encouraging for seeing their own breakthroughs that can often seem insurmountable.

Each miracle demonstrates that:
"ALL things are possible to him who believes."
Mark 9:23

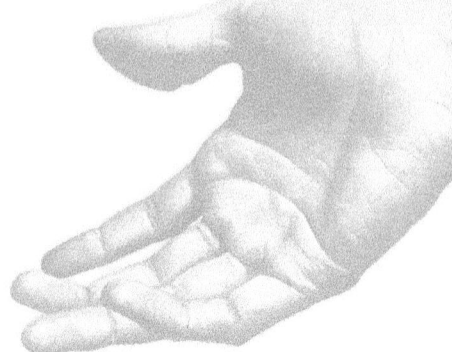

31

BLIND MAN HEALED ON THE SABBATH

John 9:1-41

APPLICATION

Are we willing to be His healing hands amid mockery, accusation and persecution? Would we regret the work and become angry with God?

Will He put to the test the depth of our love and compassion in our healing ministry with the accusation, "*Who do you think you are?*"

Uncomfortable observers hurl many accusations at the supernatural. Expect to face those taunts with victory. Silence the foe—yet love the heart behind the harsh voice.

Perhaps the accusers are in fact the neediest, more so than those with a physical need.

OBSERVATIONS OF THE BIBLICAL ACCOUNT

1. Jesus' poignant words baffled the Pharisees! Their prideful words proved to be no match for the Wisdom of the ages. Jesus' words and deeds were always very **purposeful;** He sent the blind man to a pool named "Sent" (Siloam).

2. It's interesting to note that in this account and in the prior Sabbath healing (Chapter 20, Pool of Bethesda on the Sabbath) Jesus made a point to go back and seek out the men healed, who had come under public attack. He sought them out a **second time**, to reveal Himself further. His compassion ran deeply for those being persecuted.

3. How **relentless** is the enemy to try to rob the great joy of the miracle!

COMMUNION

Open my heart, Holy Spirit, to be still and listen to Your heart. Help me to receive and believe. Prepare me for powerful new activation.

Biblical Applications and Observations

_____

_____

_____

_____

_____

_____

_____

_____

_____

_____

_____

ALONG THE WAY Reflections (on the author's story)

_____

_____

_____

_____

_____

_____

_____

_____

_____

_____

_____

CONTEMPLATIONS

Am I willing to be His healing hands amid mockery, accusation and persecution?

Would I regret the work and become angry with the Lord?

Lord, do you see any spiritual blindness in me?

Contemplations Response

_____

_____

_____

_____

_____

_____

_____

_____

_____

_____

_____

_____

Lord, what would You desire to say to me today?

_____

_____

_____

_____

_____

_____

_____

_____

_____

_____

_____

ACTIVATION PRAYER

*Lord may my **"compassion be new every morning"** as is Yours, according to Lamentations 3:23. May Your light shine brighter and brighter through me to this needy world. Grant me grace and tenacity to stomp out all the taunts of the enemy. Thank You, Lord, for this great promise in Psalm 91:13, **"You will tread on the lion and the cobra; you will trample the head of the great lion and the serpent."***

MY "ALONG THE WAY" STORIES

Keep this journal ready to fill in your stories when they happen!

"He who says he abides in Him ought...to WALK JUST AS HE WALKED."
1 John 2:6

32

MIRACLE OF IMPARTATION TO THE SEVENTY

Luke 10:1-9, 17-24

APPLICATION

As we minister more and more in the power of the Lord, He will use us to impart His anointing to others who want what we have been given. We are not to feel inadequate to do so, but rather privileged and blessed, to be awakening the fires of His Spirit in others. My husband likes to say, we are like pitchers of water, not to simply hold the water and stay full, but to be emptied for others, ready to be refilled again and again. We receive His power to then pour out for others to receive.

"Pray the Lord of the harvest to send out laborers into His harvest," (Matthew 9:38). This word by Jesus is usually misquoted. People think He said to pray for **more** workers in the harvest. No, rather He simply stated to pray He'll send them ***out!***

We have enough laborers that could advance the Kingdom, but there is little readiness to obey the *Great Commission.* It is too easy to decide that the mandate was meant for someone else more qualified, or with a special call. The truth is, we have all been commissioned:

Jesus came and spoke to them saying, **"All authority has been given to Me in heaven and on earth. Go therefore and make disciples of all the nations, baptizing them in the name of the Father and of the Son and of the Holy Spirit, teaching them to observe all things that I have commanded you; and lo, I am with you always, even to the end of the age."** (Matthew 28:18-20)

Gordon and I have been privileged to be a part of *Transform Our World*, a ministry led by Dr. Ed Silvoso of San Jose, California, for about twelve years. We have gained invaluable insights through his teachings at conferences, through his books, as well as through his friendship, to gain a vision for city, nation, and global transformation.

Around the year 2000, the Lord gave Dr. Silvoso powerful insight into the book of Luke, indicating that the tenth chapter was pivotal in His ministry. Whereas Jesus operated in a hostile spiritual climate in Chapters 1-9, after imparting His authority to the 70 (Luke 10) and sending them out ahead of Him, there was a shift to a favorable spiritual atmosphere, (up until the crucifixion). Whereas there had been much demonic activity in the beginning, there was little after this impartation to the 70.

As He granted them His authority, He also gave them *simple instructions of how to go forth* in His Name, to prepare the way for His ministry to follow. These insights are shared in Dr. Silvoso's powerful book, *Prayer Evangelism[1],* which I *highly recommend* for gaining a new lifestyle of caring and sharing along the way. *This is the only time the Lord gave such a 'how to' plan.*

The 70 were told by Jesus to:

1. **Bless** the people and households with PEACE.*
2. **Fellowship** with grace and love.
3. Meet their most pressing **"felt needs"** (miracles).
4. **Say, the Kingdom of God has come.**

Now WE are to be those sent ones!

We are to always begin with a blessing of peace! Then we are to BE a blessing, in making heart connections and releasing His love and power in breakthrough prayers. *Once we have done this, most people will be longing for what we have. . .* ***Jesus!***

The Greek word for **peace [Eirene] is used 91 times in the New Testament and is the same as the Jewish greeting "Shalom" in Hebrew. It means much more than the absence of war or turmoil. It depicts wholeness: tranquility, safety, well-being, health, contentment, success, comfort, and complete harmony with God and man.*

---

[1] Silvoso, Ed, *Prayer Evangelism: How to Change the Spiritual Climate Over Your Home, Neighborhood and City* (Ventura, CA: Regal Books, 2000, 2018). **(This book greatly impacted our lives!)**

OBSERVATIONS OF THE BIBLICAL ACCOUNT

1. Luke only recorded one miracle between my chapters of 21 and 32, of Jesus sending the Twelve, and then the Seventy. But as I have listed the miracles chronologically, it is evident that much more **time transpired** between the two impartations than would be apparent if only reading the book of Luke.

2. Knowing what a monumental day it had been for Jesus when He previously sent out the Twelve (Chapter 21) with His authority, this blessing for the 70 had been even more monumental. It set the **precedent** that His impartation of authority would be given to ALL in the church who would come to Jesus, follow and obey Him, saying *"Yes, Lord! "*

"I tell you, whoever believes in Me
will do the works I have been doing,
and they will do even GREATER THINGS than these,
because I am going to the Father."
John 14:12 NIV

COMMUNION

Open my heart, Holy Spirit, to be still and listen to Your heart. Help me to receive and believe. Prepare me for powerful new activation.

Biblical Applications and Observations

ALONG THE WAY Reflections (on the author's story)

CONTEMPLATIONS

Do I carry peace in my heart, or fear, stress, worry, and turmoil?

How consistently am I walking in my shoes of peace, enabling me to release peace along the way?

How do I seek to advance His Kingdom each day, wherever I go?

Contemplations Response

_____

_____

_____

_____

_____

_____

_____

_____

_____

_____

_____

_____

Lord, what would You desire to say to me today?

_____

_____

_____

_____

_____

_____

_____

_____

_____

_____

_____

ACTIVATION PRAYER

May Your Kingdom come out of my heart, O Lord! I honor You as the King of Kings and the Lord of Lords in my life. May You once again see satan falling like lightning around me, as I go forth on my daily assignments! May my journey of obedience and power (in the Name of Jesus) bring You great joy today, my Lord.

MY "ALONG THE WAY" STORIES

Keep this journal ready to fill in your stories when they happen!

"He who says he abides in Him ought...to WALK JUST AS HE WALKED."
1 John 2:6

33

18-YEAR INFIRMITY HEALED ON THE SABBATH

Luke 13:10-17

APPLICATION

To leave the place of faith where we once stood, but perhaps gave up over time, and to descend back into doubt is to trespass into the kingdom of darkness. **"Without faith, it is impossible to please God."** (Hebrews 11:6 NIV) With stubborn infirmities, such as this one, we must allow Him to transform our thoughts to be higher, like His. We must hear the instruction of the Master in this testimony and agree with His observation, that people are truly bound up physically by the thief who "comes to steal and kill and destroy." (John 10:10 NIV) He stated it so clearly.

Now, for the rest of the story. Also, according to John 10:10, the Master came **"that they may have life, and have it more abundantly."** *Savor this dynamic promise here!* Let's become resilient as instruments of bold faith to break the old, heavy, lingering chains we see weighing down our friends, family, and strangers. The blood of Jesus is more than enough to break every yoke of the enemy to **"set the captives free."** (Isaiah 61:1) *Think of it!*

OBSERVATIONS OF THE BIBLICAL ACCOUNT

1. I was reminded of Paul's words later, **"For the kingdom of God is not in word but in power."** (I Corinthians 4:20) Demonstrating the power and love of God to underscore His teaching, this miracle should have been considered a blessing to all, especially in the synagogue!

2. Jesus was quick to call an infirmed, stooped woman, possibly suffering rejection and shame, **"daughter of Abraham."** How lavishly He loves all of His children, and desires to honor the *least of these!*

COMMUNION

Open my heart, Holy Spirit, to be still and listen to Your heart. Help me to receive and believe. Prepare me for powerful new activation.

Biblical Applications and Observations

_____

_____

_____

_____

_____

_____

_____

_____

_____

_____

ALONG THE WAY Reflections (on the author's story)

_____

_____

_____

_____

_____

_____

_____

_____

_____

_____

CONTEMPLATIONS

Do I have a problem focus or a God focus?

What heavy burdens do I need to release to Him today?

Do I need help learning to live ABOVE everything, and not below?

Contemplations Response

Lord, what would You desire to say to me today?

ACTIVATION PRAYER

Your Kingdom come, Your will be done in and through me, O Lord! Let new faith levels explode in my life, to set the captives free. Repudiate any acceptance of entrenched strongholds impacting physical or emotional health in myself or others. Enable me to release all my heavy burdens to You, and to "walk crushing" the enemy under my feet today.

MY "ALONG THE WAY" STORIES

Keep this journal ready to fill in your stories when they happen!

"He who says he abides in Him ought...to WALK JUST AS HE WALKED."
1 John 2:6

34

DROPSY HEALED ON THE SABBATH

Luke 14:1-6

APPLICATION

Isn't the way we categorize miracles perplexing? Perhaps we can believe Him for deaf ears being opened and blind eyes seeing, but then doubt such *instant weight loss*! We think that's insignificant or even ridiculous!

Perhaps in this area we carry judgment in our hearts rather than compassion and faith. Often people with great weight issues suffer shame and are unlikely to ever ask for prayer. We may always assume there is an eating disorder, when there may be a physical disorder causing the issue.

Let's pursue God for *every issue* that does not fit into the "abundant life" that He intends. Heavy chains, heavy burdens or heavy weight physically—all are constraints to the health and freedom that He desires.

Why do we settle for less, for ourselves and for others?

OBSERVATIONS OF THE BIBLICAL ACCOUNT

1. In this case, He was in a private home of a **Pharisee**, not the synagogue. So, the man was likely a Pharisee himself, or a good friend to the religious leaders who were so against Jesus.

2. The scene must have been **super charged** in this close intimate setting!

COMMUNION

Open my heart, Holy Spirit, to be still and listen to Your heart. Help me to receive and believe. Prepare me for powerful new activation.

Biblical Applications and Observations

ALONG THE WAY Reflections (on the author's story)

CONTEMPLATIONS

What am I lacking, to walk in my abundant life?
Why do I settle for less, for myself and for others?
Do I keep on *keeping on* in the face of blind faith?

Contemplations Response

_____
_____
_____
_____
_____
_____
_____
_____
_____
_____

Lord, what would You desire to say to me today?

_____
_____
_____
_____
_____
_____
_____
_____
_____
_____
_____

ACTIVATION PRAYER

Change my heart, O Lord. Fill me with Godly compassion on my daily journey as your hands and feet. Continue to grow my understanding of this, **"with God ALL things are possible,"** *Mark 10:27. Grow my heart of expectancy to touch every need.*

MY "ALONG THE WAY" STORIES

Keep this journal ready to fill in your stories when they happen!

_____

_____

_____

_____

_____

_____

_____

_____

_____

_____

_____

_____

_____

_____

_____

_____

_____

_____

_____

"He who says he abides in Him ought...to WALK JUST AS HE WALKED."
1 John 2:6

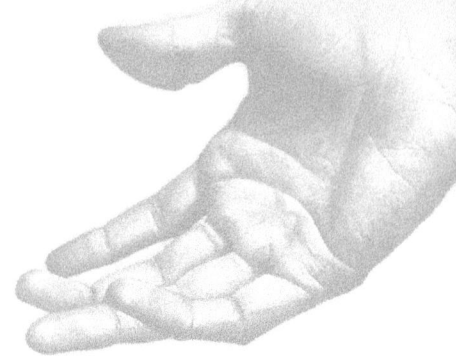

35

TEN LEPERS CLEANSED

Luke 17:11-19

APPLICATION

Heidi Baker of Mozambique has an extensive ministry to orphans, especially those on the streets.

When she finds them, she takes them in her arms and holds them for hours, until they grasp the healing love being extended to them.

She becomes their "Mama."

Her constant admonition to the body of Christ has been, *Stop for the ONE in front of you!*[1]

"Freely you have received; freely give!" (Matthew 10:8)

Whether He leads us to one or to a whole group, His power is more than enough to cover the needs of each one. I'm getting the picture of standing at the ocean with one or ten, and getting ready to go in. None would doubt there would be enough water for all ten to get wet. So great is the magnitude of His love, power, and compassion.

Let's bring them to the "Priest," our Most High God, for His mercy, love and healing!

All are worthy of our time and our love.

[1] Baker, Heidi. *Always Enough* (Ada, MI: Chosen Books, 2003)

OBSERVATIONS OF THE BIBLICAL ACCOUNT

1. As usual, Jesus was ministering along the way. He never planned a crusade or event of any kind. He simply lived to serve, every day, along the way. Should we not **adjust the frantic** pace of our lives to allow time along the way to bless people around us? It only takes a few loving words to shine the light, touch a heart, and perhaps change a life forever.

2. That day, it took only **six words to transform ten** people's lives. How amazing that He has chosen to reveal Himself to us and through us and entrust us to dispense His perfect love and power.

If only
they could know the love bursting in My heart, *the Lord said.*
My love exploded in My heart for them.
I saw each one standing there whole. . .
Let it be so in us, Lord!

COMMUNION

Open my heart, Holy Spirit, to be still and listen to Your heart. Help me to receive and believe. Prepare me for powerful new activation.

Biblical Applications and Observations

_____

_____

_____

_____

_____

_____

_____

_____

_____

_____

_____

_____

_____

ALONG THE WAY Reflections (on the author's story)

_____

_____

_____

_____

_____

_____

_____

_____

_____

_____

_____

CONTEMPLATIONS

How should I grow my flexibility to take time to bless others each day?

How can I shut down being overwhelmed by the needs of others, and only be over-whelmed by God?

How discerning am I becoming for knowing whose hearts God is wanting me to touch?

Contemplations Response

_____

_____

_____

_____

_____

_____

_____

_____

_____

_____

_____

_____

Lord, what would You desire to say to me today?

_____

_____

_____

_____

_____

_____

_____

_____

_____

_____

_____

ACTIVATION PRAYER

O Lord, grow the deep love and compassion in my heart to care when others won't, and to know there are no limits with God. Enable me to shine Your love and grace into the darkest hearts, bringing hope, healing, freedom, and joy! Make room in my heart for the masses.

MY "ALONG THE WAY" STORIES

Keep this journal ready to fill in your stories when they happen!

"He who says he abides in Him ought...to WALK JUST AS HE WALKED."
1 John 2:6

FURTHER MEDITATION: NO LIMITS

The Lord has been impressing me the last 4-5 years, that it's time to change my mindset and take the limits off. He impressed me that any thoughts of limitations do not come from Him! He inspired me to write a decree to speak over myself about this. Here are some excerpts. . .

TODAY is the day, NOW is the time, for DIVINE BREAKTHROUGH and release from the old mindset of limitations in my life.

Old limitations are being replaced today with God's divine design.

I CAN DO ALL THINGS through Christ who strengthens me!

TODAY I will operate in all things without doubt, fear, and unbelief.

The Lord Jesus is manifesting His holy nature in me, limitless and eternal.

I AM an open receiver before the Lord.

Today I AM breaking through old barriers of negativity in myself and around me (men's voices, criticism, judging, oppression, indifference of others).

God is perfecting all of this in my life NOW:

Unlimited vision/hearing—anointing to see and hear from God.
Unlimited understanding/knowledge, with downloads of the Mind of Christ.
Unlimited anointing, through Jesus the Anointed One reigning in me.
Unlimited authority and DOMINION, as it was in the beginning.
Unlimited growth and blessing of my spirit to function in new capacities.

With GOD, ALL THINGS are possible! *Hallelujah!*

36

RESURRECTION OF LAZARUS

John 11:1-54, 12:10-11

APPLICATION

In contemplating this account, I heard, *"For whoever desires to save his life will lose it, but whoever loses his life for My sake will save it."* (Luke 9:24) Our lives must be in His hands. The *length of our lives* must be in His hands; that's freedom.

There can be no insistence of *our way.* Wisdom is to want what He wants in all things. We can fully trust the One who is Perfect Love. If we can release our life and our death to Him fully, then we are free to be a living sacrifice, fully yielded, surrendered, and empowered daily to live in the supernatural. We are to faint not, whatever we must face in a day. Faith must go deeper than despair. Peace must prevail, and readiness to obey: to stay, to wait, to go. Listening is our key.

In one of my later edits, I was struck with the words of Lazarus' hands and feet being bound. This study has been about *becoming the hands and feet of Jesus.* When they are not, does the Lord see our own hands and feet bound by unbelief, apathy, timidity, or _____? *Loose us, Lord!*

OBSERVATIONS OF THE BIBLICAL ACCOUNT

1. **Only John records** this amazing event!

2. Whatever our level of faith, the Lord continuously desires to take us further. Neither the disciples, nor the sisters could **fathom** this resurrection happening, although there had been two prior resurrection miracles (Chapters 11 and 17).

Neither had happened after a lapse of so many days, however, which took the miracle and their faith to deeper levels.

COMMUNION

Open my heart, Holy Spirit, to be still and listen to Your heart. Help me to receive and believe. Prepare me for powerful new activation.

Biblical Applications and Observations

ALONG THE WAY Reflections (on the author's story)

CONTEMPLATIONS

How has my faith grown stronger in the last few months?

How can I stop putting time limits on God's miracles?

How can my faith carry me safely through my times of disappointment?

Contemplations Response

Lord, what would You desire to say to me today?

ACTIVATION PRAYER

Help me Lord to grow in listening, hearing, obeying, and trusting You, every day! Thank you for the incredible journey of grace You have designed for me. Thank You, Lord, for Your faithfulness to train me even through times of great trials, for my good and for my greatness! Enable me to always look UP and go higher over every hurdle.

MY "ALONG THE WAY" STORIES

Keep this journal ready to fill in your stories when they happen!

"He who says he abides in Him ought...to WALK JUST AS HE WALKED."
1 John 2:6

37

BLIND BARTIMAEUS AT JERICHO

Mark 10:46-52, Luke 18:35-43

APPLICATION

May we too go forth in blind faith with such bold confidence in our Lord! His call is the same to us today: *"Come!"*

Then, *"GO!"*

"But for you who revere My Name, the sun of righteousness will rise with healing in its wings. And you will go out and leap like calves released from the stall!" (Malachi 4:2)

Studying all of Jesus' miracles, we can readily observe by now that Jesus words of healing were always *simple decrees stating the breakthrough* results.

He never made petitions to the Father, asking for the healing, rather He simply released it Himself.

We are also empowered to do so, in Jesus Name, because of His indwelling presence, and His command to heal the sick. **"As you go, proclaim this message: 'The kingdom of heaven has come near.' Heal the sick, raise the dead, cleanse those who have leprosy, drive out demons. Freely you have received; freely give."** (Matthew 10:7-8)

 This is our mandate, as it was to His obedient disciples. He did not say to pray and ask Him to heal people.

He just said to do it, in His name.

OBSERVATIONS

1. Here was another instance when the blind man had already received his **spiritual vision**, because he had spiritual *ears to hear* the truth. He gave credit to Jesus as the Son of David, the lineage of the Messiah.

2. The Lord asked him what he wanted Him to do for him, obviously knowing he wanted his sight. But the **request** must first be made!

3. Although Jesus released him, "**Go your way,**" the man now chose to follow Jesus. The Lord's way had become **his way!**

COMMUNION

Open my heart, Holy Spirit, to be still and listen to Your heart. Help me to receive and believe. Prepare me for powerful new activation.

Biblical Applications and Observations

_____

_____

_____

_____

_____

_____

_____

_____

_____

_____

_____

ALONG THE WAY Reflections (on the author's story)

_____

_____

_____

_____

_____

_____

_____

_____

_____

_____

_____

_____

CONTEMPLATIONS

Do my words (in Jesus Name) have the same power as Jesus?

How am I growing to operate in my God-given authority each day?

How do I currently need to adjust my thoughts to choose His way instead of my way?

Contemplations Response

Lord, what would You desire to say to me today?

ACTIVATION PRAYER

Lord, fill my heart with overflowing faith and grace. Propel me to quickly turn as You did when a desperate cry is heard. May my heart advance readily from grace to grace, to extend your hope, love, and supernatural power wherever there is a need. Let me see more strongholds falling down like Jericho by the word of the Lord!

MY "ALONG THE WAY" STORIES

Keep this journal ready to fill in your stories when they happen!

_____

_____

_____

_____

_____

_____

_____

_____

_____

_____

_____

_____

_____

_____

_____

_____

_____

_____

_____

_____

"He who says he abides in Him ought...to WALK JUST AS HE WALKED."
1 John 2:6

Allow me to reiterate some Greek insight I shared earlier in Chapter 32. We must gain this BOLD mindset as we go forth in His Name!

Matthew 10:7 NIV states:
"As you go, proclaim this message:
'The kingdom of heaven has come near.'
Heal the sick, raise the dead."

But in the Greek, it says:
"GOING yet BE PROCLAIMING
saying that the kingdom of heaven has neared,
be CURING the infirmed...
dead ones BE ROUSING!"

Our activity in the Kingdom is to be continuous action.

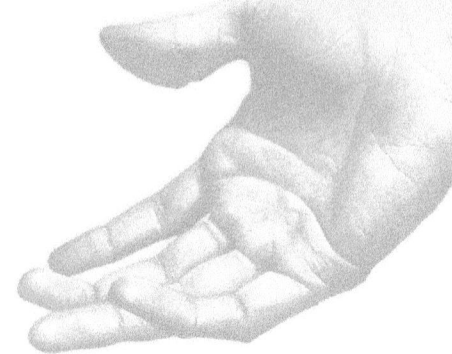

38

SOLDIER'S EAR RESTORED

Luke 22:47-53

APPLICATION

The dream was brief but pointed. When I woke and recalled the dream, I was reminded of a powerful word He had given me years ago: ***unshakable.***

"Who will you forsake? Who will you follow?"

He led me to Hebrews 12:29 which states so powerfully,

"We are receiving an unshakable kingdom."

He said to me, ***To have an unshakable kingdom, there must be unshakable people. My body must be the unshakable people of My kingdom.***

I was starting to get His point.

Then He added the clincher, ***It takes shakings to be found unshakable.***

Let's be His unshakable people!

He had once asked His disciples, **"Are you still so dull?"** (Matthew 15:16)

Clearly, they were still clueless at times!

Here they were, caving to fear, though He had often taught them to *fear not!*

Love was to be their only motive if they were to truly follow Him.

OBSERVATIONS

1. **Only** Dr. Luke disclosed this healing! The other three simply relayed the ear being *cut off.* (Only John described the unusual manifestation of Jesus' power that caused some of His captors to fall to the ground.)

2. Emotions would likely still be unnerving, even 30 years later, when the first gospel had been written. Their stunned reaction to Jesus' arrest would forever **imprint** their remembrance of that fateful night in the two gardens.

3. Jesus demonstrated flawless **humility** to entreat His disciples to "permit" Him to do what He wanted to do! [Greek: permit; not to restrain.] He didn't need His own disciples to stand in the way of what would be His last incredible compassion miracle prior to the cross—still demonstrating what He had always taught.

"Love your enemy. . .
and if your enemy strikes you on one side,
turn the other cheek."
Matthew 5:39, 43

Jesus would not compromise His heart of compassion and grace,
even in the face of imminent danger.

COMMUNION

Open my heart, Holy Spirit, to be still and listen to Your heart. Help me to receive and believe. Prepare me for powerful new activation.

Biblical Applications and Observations

_____

_____

_____

_____

_____

_____

_____

_____

_____

_____

_____

_____

_____

ALONG THE WAY Reflections (on the author's story)

_____

_____

_____

_____

_____

_____

_____

_____

_____

_____

_____

_____

_____

CONTEMPLATIONS

Who will I forsake? Who will I follow?
How can I grow in loving my enemies?
Have I been turning the other cheek?

Contemplations Response

Lord, what would You desire to say to me today?

ACTIVATION PRAYER

Lord, in the face of any danger or persecution, may Your perfect Love cast out all fear in my heart. I choose to daily submit in obedience to Your ways. Enable me to love my enemies with a deeply radical heart of compassion flowing freely from You to me, to my world.

MY "ALONG THE WAY" STORIES

Keep this journal ready to fill in your stories when they happen!

"He who says he abides in Him ought...to WALK JUST AS HE WALKED."
1 John 2:6

FURTHER MEDITATION: FEAR NOT

Most people have heard it taught that the Bible says to "fear not" 365 times. Obviously, that should tell us that on any day, no matter what comes, we are to "fear not!"

Fear is one of the most powerful tactics of the enemy to defeat us, to block our faith and trust in God, amidst life's difficulties.

I've heard it taught that sin is rebellion, stemming from three roots: **pride, fear, and unbelief**. It seems to be true. This infers that all other sins are merely branches on the tree of rebellion. *We must tackle those roots!*

About 10 years ago, the Lord told me He wanted to give me a "no fear anointing." It's a long story, which I won't share here, but He convinced me that fear must be shut down. It defeats us and puts us in a self-reliant state, when in fact, we can always trust God to do His job. I'm not saying we are not to make unwise or careless choices, but there is a huge shift in attitudes most of us need to make. I did.

We can stand in the face of danger and have great confidence, when perhaps no one else will. We do not have to fall apart! That's what we see here in Jesus. He wasn't fearful for self-preservation. He stood His ground in faith, trust, love, and mercy in the face of grave danger.

"There is no fear in love. But perfect love drives out fear because fear has to do with punishment. The one who fears is not made perfect in love." (1 John 4:18 NIV)

"For I am the LORD your God who takes hold of your right hand and says to you, Do not fear; I will help you." (Isaiah 41:13 NIV)

"So we say with confidence, "The Lord is my helper; I will not be afraid. What can mere mortals do to me?" (Hebrew 13:6)

"I sought the LORD, and He answered me; He delivered me from all my fears." (Psalms 34:4 NIV) *That was written by a giant slayer!*

Look up more! Confess and repent. Choose to live FREE of fear and let Him also give you His NO FEAR ANOINTING! (Label worry for what it is, fear!)

FEAR NOT!

39

RESURRECTION OF JESUS!

Matt 28:1-10, Mark 16:1-8, Luke 24:1-12, 25-46, John 20:1-18

APPLICATION

The Lord ministered to His fearful disciples when He appeared to them, in the exact same way He had instructed the "Seventy" in Luke 10. *See Chapter 32, regarding "Prayer Evangelism."*

1. He came speaking **peace!**
2. He **fellowshipped** with them—lingering and eating fish and honeycomb.
3. He ministered to their **needs**—reassuring them and instructing them.
4. He brought the **Kingdom of God** to them!

Apart from the above, how are we to apply the resurrection element ourselves?

"Then He said to them, '**If anyone desires to come after Me, let him deny himself, and take up his cross daily, and follow Me. For whoever desires to save his life will lose it, but whoever loses his life for My sake will save it.'**" (Luke 9:23-24)

"**I want to know Christ—yes, to know the power of his resurrection and participation in his sufferings, becoming like him in his death, and so, somehow, attaining to the resurrection from the dead.**" (Philippians 3:10-11 NIV)

We too are equipped and commanded to walk in this same amazing lifestyle of power and victory over the enemy. The resident life of Jesus in us is to be poured out of us in His unfathomable power. Beyond our own dying to self and overcoming lifestyle, we are also to believe He can use any of us to release resurrection power for the dead!

OBSERVATIONS OF THE BIBLICAL ACCOUNT

1. Prior to the cross He had *prophesied His death and resurrection* clearly to them on several occasions.

Matthew 20:18-19, **"Behold, we are going up to Jerusalem, and the Son of Man will be betrayed to the chief priests and to the scribes; and they will condemn Him to death and deliver Him to the Gentiles to mock and to scourge and to crucify. And <u>the third day He will rise again</u>."** (See also Luke 9:22.)

2. Those words were spoken so clearly to prepare them, but they did **not have ears to hear.**

A VISION

I'd been enjoying the Lord's perfect love and embrace at the Throne Room when He swooped me up and carried me away as a child. Up, up, up we ascended far above the scene below and found ourselves in utter darkness. I felt completely safe in His arms.

A cross suddenly appeared before us and I knew it was intended for crucifixion. I never expected His next words and felt no emotions until the end, as it all happened so fast.

Lovingly, the Lord spoke to me with a lilt in His voice, **Hop on!**

What?! I then saw *myself* hanging on the cross, in modern-day clothes without any blood.

After a few seconds, my body metamorphosed into a bare white skeleton! *What?!*

After a few more seconds, the white bones turned to a dazzling gold skeleton hanging on that cross! *What in the world??!!*

Lastly, a new body in a white robe appeared briefly on the cross then flew off into the distance, as if on a mission. The cross disappeared. The Lord simply told me, **You have been crucified with Me and resurrected, and now you live a resurrected life.**

He carried me back down to the Throne Room where I reflected on this vision and grasped this reality in a brand new way. He wants us to know we are to live *in the power of the resurrection!*

I would never forget this reality which had seemed so vague before. My heart felt like it was pumping hard with love, grace, gratitude and awe. *Thank You, Lord!*

Note: The golden skeleton apparently indicates that the very moment we are born again, we step into a realm of royalty that we have likely never understood.

COMMUNION

Open my heart, Holy Spirit, to be still and listen to Your heart. Help me to receive and believe. Prepare me for powerful new activation.

Biblical Applications and Observations

_____

_____

_____

_____

_____

_____

_____

_____

_____

_____

_____

_____

ALONG THE WAY Reflections (on the author's story)

_____

_____

_____

_____

_____

_____

_____

_____

_____

_____

_____

_____

CONTEMPLATIONS

How do I see myself growing as a listener to what He is saying?

How stubborn is my faith, hope, and love?

Do I pay close attention to the prophetic words of the Lord to me?

Contemplations Response

Lord, what would You desire to say to me today?

ACTIVATION PRAYER

Enable me, Lord, to fear not and faint not in the face of any adversity or confusion. Thank you for Your strength in my weakness, to stand firm in my faith, despite any persecution or threat. Open my ears to grow in hearing You more clearly. I receive the grace to be immovable and unshakable, that I will not shrink back, but will press on to stand in victory and boldness.

MY "ALONG THE WAY" STORIES

Keep this journal ready to fill in your stories when they happen!

"He who says he abides in Him ought...to WALK JUST AS HE WALKED."
1 John 2:6

FURTHER MEDITATION: HIS SACRIFICE

For those who only purchase the book, but not this journal, they will miss one of my most amazing miracles to this point. This is another personal testimony in my life, one which occurred after compiling all my "Along the Way" stories, so it seemed best to include it here.

I thoroughly enjoyed the afternoon at the house of a dear friend. When he demonstrated a quick ride on their backyard zipline, it looked like fun and I wanted to try it. I had been on two serious ziplines overseas in the Caribbean and in Mexico and loved it both times. This one was much smaller, about 12-14 feet high and 100 ft long. He was hesitant but agreed. Their family had installed it about six months prior, and all had enjoyed it greatly.

Excitedly, I climbed up and mounted it in a standing position, holding onto the T-bar handle. Off I went, whirring down the line. However, all at once, only about 6-7 feet from the start, the handles on the T-bar, much like bike grips, both decided to come completely off! That had never happened before! Immediately I took a headfirst backwards dive to the ground, as one of his kids filmed me.

It happened so fast that I had no time to be afraid. I hit the ground in no time. What made no sense in the natural was that at the last couple of seconds, my vertical descent suddenly shifted, so that I landed on my back, with my feet straight up in the air. The back of my head made contact and bounced twice, but not hard. The owner felt more shocked than I did.

I had no pain! I slowly turned my head side to side and moved my arms and legs in various directions. I waited a few minutes, as they prayed over me, and still had no pain or dizziness.

Hey, I'm getting up. God protected me!

They were leery of me moving like that but could tell I seemed fine. So, I got up and walked into the house. I still had no pain. They quickly tended to a couple of scratches on my back and two small cuts and prayed over me again. At their insistence, I laid down for about 30 minutes. My only discomfort seemed to be some minor tightness in my upper leg joints, but nothing to slow me down. Soon I got up and drove home.

We all knew I had been given an incredible miracle of God's protection. My life was spared, as well as all my bones, joints, muscles, and ligaments. I never even had any bruising. *How could this ever be possible?!*

Later that day a single missionary gal with a healing ministry (Trina) texted me to request a place to stay the next day. She had never done that before, though she had a standing invitation. I smiled, immediately realizing that God wanted to reassure me even more, by sending someone with a global healing ministry! She's also very prophetic.

The next day I awoke with no soreness or pain. I felt about 95%, with only the tightness in my upper leg joints. When Trina arrived, I told her nothing. After a while I mentioned that there had been an odd incident the day before and asked if she would like to ask the Lord to show her anything about what had happened.

Sure! She always loved a prophetic challenge.

After she prayed and listened a moment, she said she kept seeing me laying in the hand of Jesus, like He had caught me! The hand of Jesus (that my daughter-in-law had drawn for this book and journal) hung on the wall in our guest house, right over my shoulder where we were sitting. *Yes!*

That explained it! That's why my position had changed, just as I landed. He caught me! Otherwise, the outcome would have been quite different, had I landed directly on my head as it looked like I would have in the video.

Though He protected my life, I felt something quite odd afterwards for several weeks. I kept getting the feeling I had passed from death to life. It's like I had a new lease on life, due to His amazing watchcare of love and grace in His miraculous protection. Then one day, He revealed what had happened, in one simple statement.

I died that you might live, I heard.

Oh! Of course, You did! THANK YOU!

The reality of that took on a whole new meaning, now. He took my death.

"I have been crucified with Christ
And I no longer live, but Christ lives in me.
The life I now live in the body,
I live by faith in the Son of God,
Who loved me and gave Himself for me.
Galatians 2:20

My life is not my own.

"He died for all,
that those who live
should live no longer for themselves,
but for Him who died for them
and rose on their behalf."
2 Corinthians 5:15

Do you know this for your life?

40

ANOTHER MIRACULOUS CATCH OF FISH

John 21:1-25

APPLICATION

We must stay close to our Lord! We must not turn away in fear or rebellion. However, should we do so, we too are being invited by Perfect Love, Grace, and Mercy to jump back into the Living Waters and swim. We are to jump into the deep, with no holding back!

Wherever we are in our journey, we are invited to come closer.
Mercy waits to greet us.

The Father, Son, and Holy Spirit want to give us each a life message that cannot be stopped. Love has called us, and Life has equipped us. Let us go forth in His powerful Name and learn to be great fishers of men.

As followers of the Lord, just like Peter, James, John, Matthew, the Marys and others, *we have work to do. We must go fishing for the hearts of men,* women, and children. How? With nets of love, just like Jesus!

He brought the miracle catch that day
to catch the heart of Peter again
with His incredible heart of mercy.

OBSERVATIONS

God continually amazed me throughout this study!

1. I had **John 21:25** in mind throughout the entire study to use at the end, *but I had no idea it stands as the last verse in this last miracle account!* The Lord knew what great **confirmation** to my heart that would be that He had been guiding me all along.

2. I noticed the disciples did not leave their nets this time. Apparently, they were again drawing **security** from those nets, and even the miraculous catch. They counted every last slippery fish! Fishing for men did not seem to be on their minds.

3. This was the only time we are told that Jesus cooked a meal for them. If it was indeed the first time He did, it may have reminded them of the time He washed their feet. Their Master who appeared even greater in their eyes now, having died and now resurrected—now chose to **humbly** serve them once again!

"And there are also many other things that Jesus did,
which if they were written one by one,
I suppose that even the world itself
could not contain the books that would be written."
John 21:25

COMMUNION

Open my heart, Holy Spirit, to be still and listen to Your heart. Help me to receive and believe. Prepare me for powerful new activation.

Biblical Applications and Observations

_____

_____

_____

_____

_____

_____

_____

_____

_____

_____

_____

_____

ALONG THE WAY Reflections (on the author's story)

_____

_____

_____

_____

_____

_____

_____

_____

_____

_____

_____

CONTEMPLATIONS

How can I perfect my heart to value LOVE as the greatest miracle to pursue and release?

How can I train my eyes to focus on Him more clearly each day?

How open am I to hear the Lord redefining His calling for me ?

Contemplations Response

Lord, what would You desire to say to me today?

ACTIVATION PRAYER

Thank You for Your amazing call to me to "follow You," and be a "fisher of men." Saturate me with your love that I may BE LOVE in this hurting world. Use me! Have your way. Use my eyes, my lips, my time, my hands and my feet to catch, bless and heal countless hearts and lives in Your unbreakable net of love.

MY "ALONG THE WAY" STORIES

Keep this journal ready to fill in your stories when they happen!

_____

_____

_____

_____

_____

_____

_____

_____

_____

_____

_____

_____

_____

_____

_____

_____

_____

_____

_____

_____

"He who says he abides in Him ought...to WALK JUST AS HE WALKED."
1 John 2:6

THANK YOU!

I am blessed that you have chosen to take this journey with me!

I commend you for pursuing this deeper walk with the Lord, to become His hands and feet. We know that is His plan for all His followers, yet not all are ready, or understand.

He has made you and I ready. He has our *YES!*

Perhaps you have seen some miracles already, but perhaps not.

If you have not yet prayed with a stranger, simply go for it. It gets easier every time. The hindrance to that is actually a heart issue, not being compelled in love, despite feelings of inadequacy.

Perhaps fear is still the culprit. *What if nothing happens?*

Let me tell you; *something always happens!* Your love has touched their heart! At times, people are moved to tears, simply by the prayer, even if nothing changes yet physically.

Recently when we offered prayer for our Russian waitress, her mouth fell open, and she exclaimed, *"For FREE?!! Never before has this happened!!"* She could not have been happier.

Also, remember that "perfect love casts out fear," (1 John 4:18.) It's best to go on the offense, to overcome that stronghold. In the morning when you start your day, tell the Lord, "Today I choose to walk in freedom over fear. Perfect my love today. Thank You that *'perfect love casts out fear.'* Today I will be obedient to Your leading." Then when the time comes, say "YES LORD," and *don't debate!* Ask others to pray over you for this.

Wherever you are on your journey, be expectant!

---

*"But to you who fear My name, the Sun of Righteousness shall arise
with healing in His wings, and you shall go out. . ."*
Malachi 4:2

EPILOGUE

This concludes the original 40 miracles of Jesus that we are to emulate in various ways, to magnify His Name. Thank you for going on this extensive spiritual journey of miracles with me!

My hope has been that as we follow Him and carefully observe His love and miracle working power, we would go and do likewise, as His hands and feet.

It is clear He wants to use us. *It's either us, His body, residing here on earth, or no one!* That includes all of us who WILL.

There are other supernatural events recorded in the Bible that did not seem applicable for the purposes of this book.

After working on the manuscript off and on for several years, I finally finished the 40 chapters. They were all typed and ready to take along on a trip across the country, where a dear friend would receive the manuscript to edit.

About one week before that trip, the Lord surprised me by bringing up the following five events, with instructions to add them at the end of the book.

Really?!

Though none of them seemed like ones to emulate, He was quick to convey the applications that He had for me to glean and share.

It all made sense then.

Be ready to stretch your faith even more!
Here is the Lord's bonus section for you!

HIS HANDS, MY FEET

JOURNAL

PART 2

1

SUDDEN BOAT TRANSPORT

John 6:16-21

APPLICATION

Let the Lord take all the limits off and give us a new mindset.

*What does He **not** have dominion over?* **Nothing.**

*What do we **not** have dominion over?* **Nothing.**

*What is He **not** willing to do?* **Nothing.**

This book has been about being *the hands and feet of Jesus*, to do the miracles He did. Though this story was not on my list to be included, He wanted it to be.

He wants us to know that when a transport miracle is needed, we may just find it happening. Yes, it is happening today. I have read several accounts around the world, though they are still not commonplace.

The point is, we need to take off all limits regarding our faith in His supernatural ways, as I shared in Further Meditation, Chapter 35.

Lift us up Lord, ever higher in our faith and our activation!

His ways are not our ways; they are higher!
see Isaiah 55:8-9

OBSERVATIONS

1. According to the *Chronological Study Bible* by Thomas Nelson, this boat miracle is the conclusion to the same event, when Peter walked on the water in Mark 4:35-41 and Matthew 8: 23-27. Strangely this part of the story was omitted in those two accounts.

   On the other hand, John himself omits Peter walking on the water. This helps us grasp why God called forth **four sets of eyes** to tell the life story of Jesus, through Matthew, Mark, Luke, and John.

2. This had **not been the first time** in the Bible there was a transport miracle, and it would not be the last.

[Greek: *harpazzo*. To transport; suddenly taken.]

Elijah outran Ahab's chariot for 14 miles back to town after the slaying of the 900 prophets of Baal on Mt Carmel. A chariot can go about 35-40 mph, while an average man can only run about 15 mph. So, he was given divine strength to run at least twice the normal speed, while holding up his heavy garments that were surely flapping in the breeze!

"Then the hand of the Lord came upon Elijah;
and he girded up his loins
and ran AHEAD of Ahab to the entrance of Jezreel."
1 Kings 18:46

COMMUNION

Open my heart, Holy Spirit, to be still and listen to Your heart. Help me to receive and believe. Prepare me for powerful new activation.

Biblical Applications and Observations

ALONG THE WAY Reflections (on the author's story)

CONTEMPLATIONS

How can I proactively submit all my commuting and travelling time more carefully to Him?

How can I increase my faith to stop limiting certain things in the Bible to "those other people" but not me?

How can I better allow my faith to freefall into His ways, His will without old restrictive mindsets?

Contemplations Response

_____

_____

_____

_____

_____

_____

_____

_____

_____

_____

Lord, what would You desire to say to me today?

_____

_____

_____

_____

_____

_____

_____

_____

_____

ACTIVATION PRAYER

*Lord, I choose to say **no** to all the places where limitations have been lodging mentally for years in my mind, to completely shut them down.*

I am saying "NO" to limits and "YES" to Your supernatural and unpredictable ways. *Increase my faith to both dislodge and catapult the faith of others, to new heights.*

*Use my journey with You to demonstrate that **"with God, all things are possible!"*** (Matthew 19:26b)

MY "ALONG THE WAY" STORIES

Keep this journal ready to fill in your stories when they happen!

_____

_____

_____

_____

_____

_____

_____

_____

_____

_____

_____

_____

_____

_____

_____

_____

_____

_____

"He who says he abides in Him ought...to WALK JUST AS HE WALKED."
1 John 2:6

FURTHER MEDITATION: DARE TO DREAM

A world-renowned speaker, Graham Cooke (Brilliant Perspectives, California) shared that when He was getting ready to speak one time, the Lord had him stop and ask an unexpected question to the audience. "Who is waiting to see a dream unfold?" When he did, only the hands of those in college and younger raised their hands. He realized that all the others had quit dreaming.

Yes, the Lord spoke to his heart, *my people have quit dreaming.*

The Lord told him to start teaching people to start dreaming again.

When we read of an unusual miracle like this boat transport, most of us automatically put it in the category of, *that would never happen to me.*

Or why would He ever do that in my life? **Why not?**

God wants the supernatural to invade every part of our lives. He wants to overlay His SUPER onto everything NATURAL. Let's believe Him for that! As we do, we will find ourselves walking in the supernatural in increasing measure. If we always doubt that could happen, it's likely nothing will.

"I will pour out My Spirit on all flesh; your sons and your daughters shall prophesy, your old men shall dream dreams, your young men shall see visions." (Joel 2:28)

Never stop dreaming and believing God for the NEW!

God is always supernatural.
The more we yield to Him, and release old mindsets,
the more supernatural our lives will become.

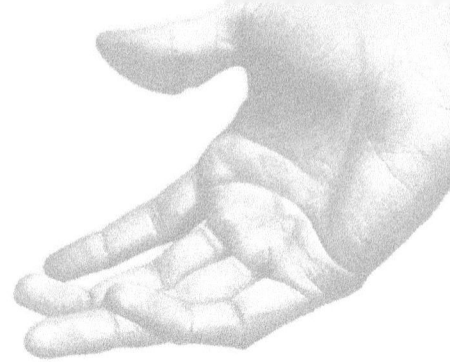

2

TRANSFIGURATION

Matthew 17:1-13

APPLICATIONS

The Lord surprisingly gave me four distinct aspects to consider, whereas I had originally thought there was no way to "apply" the transfiguration to our lives. Please realize that in this setting, these can only be touchpoints, and not an exhaustive unpacking of these matters. Hopefully, these will be a catalyst to seek more from the Lord for your own life applications.

Here is what He gave me:

1. Glory to Glory
2. Shining Transformation
3. Eyes and Ears Opened
4. Bring Others UP!

Amazing, isn't it? Let's look at each of the four applications.

APPLICATION 1: GLORY TO GLORY

We now have the indwelling Holy Spirit living within us. According to His Word, we have already been given a position in glory, though we may not have yet grasped this significant reality. **"And God raised us up with Christ and seated us with Him in the heavenly realms in Christ Jesus."** (Ephesians 2:6 NIV)

"But our citizenship is in heaven." (Philippians 3:20) We are now citizens of heaven! Really! Meditate on this. Recently the Lord surprised me as He began speaking to me *every morning* about this Holy mandate, ***Take your rightful place!*** These were the verses He brought to mind. He meant for me to take my God-given place at the throne with Him. He blew my mind that first day, because I knew He meant business. As He continued to awaken me that way for about a month, I soon realized He intended for this to be my new-normal place of abiding in Him! So, I daily let Him mentally (and visually) draw me UP to be seated with Him in the throne room. In this study, He has impressed me that it is a subsequent mode of the blessing He gave Peter, James and John up on the mountain, transcending the earthly realm as they had always known it. This vantage point of victory from which to pray is available to every believer. This is such good news, and yet we have missed it—for the most part—in our experience. Once we discover our place, we should start shouting our accolades like Peter, **"Lord, this is so awesome that we can be here!"**

APPLICATION 2: SHINING TRANSFORMATION

He reminded me of a verse He gave me about twenty years ago. Psalm 34:5 says, **"Those who look to Him are radiant; their faces are never covered with shame!"** At the time, I remember thinking it would only take one hand to name people I would call radiant! *Lord, help us!*

Pastor Dave Wilkerson, who founded the Times Square Church in New York City, once preached a sermon entitled, "We Need to Get Our Faces Saved!" The Lord told me another time that the key plan for my life, in just one word was—***Shine!*** I loved hearing that simple plan because I could remember it easily. However, it can be challenging to learn to consistently live that way. God has given that admonition to all of us in Isaiah 60:1, **"Arise, shine, for your light has come, and the glory of the Lord rises upon you!"** Thankfully, it came with a promise of grace and glory!

APPLICATION 3: EYES AND EARS OPENED

Our God wants to open the eyes and ears for all His people, to see and hear the supernatural aspects of His Kingdom. According to Acts 10:34, **"He is no respecter of persons,"** though we tend to think He is. Let me encourage you to shift your thinking and *be expectant!* Press in for more flow of His supernatural revelations! Just as we ask Him for ears to hear, we should also be asking for spiritual eyes to see. Jesus said in Matthew 11:15, **"Whoever has ears, let them hear."** Elisha prayed for his servant's eyes in 2 Kings 6:17, **"Open his eyes, O Lord that he may see. Then the Lord opened the servant's eyes, and he looked and saw the hills full of horses and chariots of fire all around them."**

In my Preface to this book, I shared that I when I asked the Lord to give me *ears to hear Him speak about the gospel stories*, His Spirit also challenged me to ask for *eyes to see into the gospel stories*. He amazed me in doing so! If you think you cannot hear or see, *break agreement with the enemy that you can't* and start thanking God that He will do a new thing. Believe and receive! You may need to ask someone to pray over you for this if you are discouraged in this area—someone who can already see and hear well.

APPLICATION 4: BRING OTHERS UP HIGHER

In this book about *being the hands and feet of Jesus*, this is another way we are to do so, to bring other believers up to the high places of communion and intercession that we have learned to frequent! We are to let others see and hear us flow in His Spirit and help them to operate in ways they never thought possible. For example, when we are able to grow in taking our *rightful place*, as in Application 1 (above), invite others to pray with you to hear and observe how you commune in this way.

When you begin to see visions, encourage others and pray over them to also learn to see. Our own journey is always intended to help others grow as well. We certainly don't want to share our new experiences in such a way that puts ourselves on a pedestal, but to encourage others to grow in learning the same thing, and to give them our helpful encouragement. As we flow in the spirit in new ways, we have a new blessing or anointing that we can pass onto others, with the laying on of hands, and anointing with oil. Let them know you will be excited to hear their stories, as they begin to unfold for them in new ways.

OBSERVATIONS OF THE BIBLICAL ACCOUNT

1. The disciples were **strangely silent** in asking Jesus anything about this incredible glorious event, or even expressing any gratitude for this unheard-of honor and privilege. Their only question was regarding the Old Testament prophecy about Elijah returning.

2. Jesus invited his closest followers into an experience they did not even request. He will also **surprise** us at times, also with His holy invitations.

COMMUNION

Open my heart, Holy Spirit, to be still and listen to Your heart. Help me to receive and believe. Prepare me for powerful new activation.

Biblical Applications and Observations

ALONG THE WAY Reflections (on the author's story)

CONTEMPLATIONS

How willing am I to shift from my regular prayer mode, to take my rightful place of authority in the heavenlies?

What attitudes do I need to alter, so others would consider me peaceful, joyful and radiant?

How am I carefully growing my ears to hear and eyes to see?

Contemplations Response

_____

_____

_____

_____

_____

_____

_____

_____

_____

_____

Lord, what would You desire to say to me today?

_____

_____

_____

_____

_____

_____

_____

_____

_____

_____

ACTIVATION PRAYER

Lord, activate me as a citizen of heaven, to abide here and there with You. Enable me to bring others UP with me, to take their rightful place, to commune and reign with You. Thank you, Lord for Your amazing glory, arising over me, that I may SHINE with the radiance of Your presence!

According to Psalm 16:11, **"in Your presence is fullness of joy!"**

MY "ALONG THE WAY" STORIES

Keep this journal ready to fill in your stories when they happen!

"He who says he abides in Him ought...to WALK JUST AS HE WALKED."
1 John 2:6

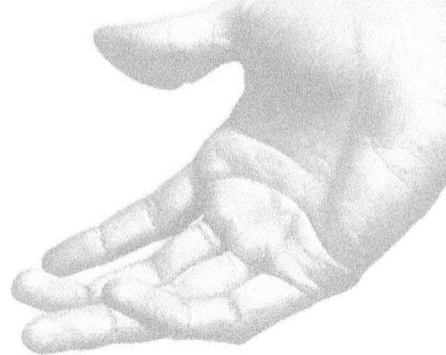

3

CURSING OF THE FIG TREE

Matthew 21:18-22, Mark 11:12-25

APPLICATION

The *new faith challenge* our Lord spoke to His disciples is one of the most significant teachings He had given them. That is why this event had to be included in this book on miracles.

First, He gave an example of Kingdom authority over creation, even though figs were out of season. We are to be fruitful and ready **"in season and out of season."** (2 Timothy 4:2) We need to ask Him to show us personally what that looks like.

Then Jesus gave instructions to really go for it, in their authority over creation. *Look at that fig tree through the eyes of Peter!* It seemed preposterous what happened that day. But Jesus chose the preposterous to predicate the words He was about to speak on faith and authority.

Our positional authority actually began at our rebirth into the second Adam and awaits our discovery. We are in Him, and He is in us, but sadly, we barely reveal Him!

Jesus says to us:

"Have faith in God. . . If anyone says to this mountain,
'Go, throw yourself into the sea,' and does not doubt in their heart
but believes that what they say will happen, it will be done for them.
Therefore, I tell you, whatever you ask for in prayer, believe that you
have received it, and it will be yours." Mark 11:22-24 NIV

OBSERVATIONS OF THE BIBLICAL ACCOUNT

1. *It was not the season for figs.*

    This unusual action (cursing) of the Lord had been sandwiched between two high profile events: His triumphal entry into Jerusalem and the overturning of the tables in the temple. **None of these events** fit into the disciples' newfound understanding of His supernatural ways.

2. The fact is, He only did what **He saw His Father do.** *Perhaps the Lord was surprised as well,* at some of the leadings of the Father, by the Spirit. And yet, His perfect obedience proved itself, over and over.

"Most assuredly, I say to you the Son can do nothing of Himself, but
what He sees the Father do; for whatever He does,
the Son also does in like manner."
John 5:19

COMMUNION

Open my heart, Holy Spirit, to be still and listen to Your heart. Help me to receive and believe. Prepare me for powerful new activation.

Biblical Applications and Observations

ALONG THE WAY Reflections (on the author's story)

CONTEMPLATIONS

Do I usually balk or do I obey when the ways of the Lord seem preposterous?

How am I guarding against judging God for His actions?

How willing am I to step into my authority regarding His creation?

Contemplations Response

Lord, what would You desire to say to me today?

ACTIVATION PRAYER

Lord, capture my heart with deep conviction of new realms of faith You are ready to pour into my daily journey with You. Enable me to see and do things in the Name of Jesus, I never before thought possible! Use my own words of blessing to impact all of creation where I live.

MY "ALONG THE WAY" STORIES

Keep this journal ready to fill in your stories when they happen!

_____

_____

_____

_____

_____

_____

_____

_____

_____

_____

_____

_____

_____

_____

_____

_____

_____

_____

_____

"He who says he abides in Him ought...to WALK JUST AS HE WALKED."
1 John 2:6

"For the creation waits
in eager expectation
for the children of God to be revealed.

For the creation was subjected to frustration,
not by its own choice,
but by the will of the one who subjected it,
in hope that the creation itself
will be liberated
from its BONDAGE to DECAY
and brought into the freedom and glory
of the children of God.

We know that the whole creation
has been groaning as in the pains of childbirth,
right up to the present time."
Romans 8:19-22 (NIV)

NOW IS THE TIME
for us to walk in our God-given authority
over all creation!

4

JESUS' CRUCIFIXION

Matthew 27:32-56, Mark 15:16-32, Luke 23:26-43,
John 19:16-27

APPLICATION

In the beginning of Jesus' ministry, He spoke two poignant words to a few chosen ones, *Follow me!*

Whenever I consider those simple words spoken to some potential disciples, I reflect on this: They could not have known that day that those two words would propel them to the scene of a cross, both His and theirs.

As we contemplate the necessity of Jesus' powerful life being displayed in overcoming death, we must realize it is the same for us. Let us not be shortsighted. Then Jesus said to his disciples, **"Whoever wants to be my disciple must deny themselves and take up their cross and follow me. For whoever wants to save their life will lose it, but whoever loses their life for me will find it."** (Matthew 16:24-25 NIV)

And yet, any form of dying, whether sacrificing our wants, serving others, suffering, or even facing physical death, seems to find most of us with complaining, doubting, questioning, and squirming in discomfort. Let us stop squirming and YIELD fully to LIVE fully.

Where is our joyful journey, our peace in the storm, and our victory?

"Don't you know that what you sow in the ground doesn't germinate unless it dies? And what you sow is not the body that will come into being, but the bare seed. And it's hard to tell whether it's wheat or some other seed. But when it dies, God

gives it a <u>new form</u>, a body to <u>fulfill his purpose</u>, and He sees to it that each seed gets a new body of its own and becomes the plant He designed it to be . . .

·. . . It is <u>sown in weakness but will be raised in power</u>.

If there is a physical body, there is also a spiritual body. For it is written: The first man, Adam, became a living soul. The last Adam became the life-giving Spirit. However, the spiritual didn't come first. The natural precedes the spiritual.

The first man was from the dust of the earth; the second Man is the Lord Jehovah, from the realm of heaven. The first one, made from dust, has a race of people just like him, who are also made from dust. The One sent from heaven has a race of heavenly people who are just like him.

> *Once we carried the likeness of the man of dust,*
> *but now let us carry the likeness of the Man of heaven.*

. . . But we thank God for giving us the victory as conquerors through our Lord Jesus, the Anointed One. So now, beloved ones stand firm and secure. Live your lives with an unshakable confidence.

We know that we prosper and excel in every season by serving the Lord, because we are assured that our union with the Lord makes our labor productive with fruit that endures." (1 Corinthians 15:34-38, 44-49, 57-58 TPT)

OBSERVATIONS OF THE BIBLICAL ACCOUNT

I am using the four Gospel writers to share their **unique** observations, instead of mine:

1. Brother Matthew: **"The chief priests mocked him, 'He saved others, but He can't save Himself. . .Let Him come down now from the cross, and we will believe in Him' . . . Jesus cried out in a loud voice, 'My God, My God, why have You forsaken Me?' . . . The earth shook, the rocks split . . .The centurion and the guards were terrified, 'Surely He was the Son of God!'"**
    (Matthew 27:42, 46, 51-52, 54 NIV)

2. Brother Mark: **"Pilate asked Him, 'Are you the King of the Jews?'. . . 'You have said so,' Jesus replied . . . Pilate wanted to satisfy the crowd . . . 'Crucify Him,' they shouted. . . A company of soldiers struck Him on the head again and again with a staff and spit on Him. Falling on their knees, they paid [mock] homage to Him . . . With a loud cry, Jesus breathed His last. The curtain of the temple was torn in two from top to bottom."** (Mark 15:2, 13, 15, 19, 37-38 NIV)

3. Dr. Luke: **"As the soldiers led Him away. . .a large number of people followed Him, including women who mourned and wailed for Him. Jesus turned and said, 'Daughters of Jerusalem, do not weep for Me; weep for yourselves and your children'. . . At the place called the Skull, they crucified Him . . . Jesus said, 'Father, forgive them, for they do not know what they are doing'. . . the sun stopped shining . . .Jesus called out with a loud voice, 'Father into your hands I commit My spirit' . . .and He breathed His last."** (Luke 23:26-28, 33-24, 45-46 NIV)

4. Brother John: **"Pilate took Jesus and had Him flogged. The soldiers twisted together a crown of thorns and put it on His head. They clothed Him in a purple robe and said again and again, 'Hail, King of the Jews,' and they slapped Him in the face . . . Later, Jesus said, 'I am thirsty'. . . they soaked a sponge with [wine vinegar]. . . on a stalk of hyssop . . . When He had received the drink, Jesus said, 'IT IS FINISHED' and gave up His spirit."** (John 19:1-3, 28-30 NIV)

COMMUNION

Open my heart, Holy Spirit, to be still and listen to Your heart. Help me to receive and believe. Prepare me for powerful new activation.

Biblical Applications and Observations

_____

_____

_____

_____

_____

_____

_____

_____

_____

_____

_____

_____

ALONG THE WAY Reflections (on the author's story)

_____

_____

_____

_____

_____

_____

_____

_____

_____

_____

_____

_____

CONTEMPLATIONS

How faithfully am I willing to follow Him, wherever He leads?

How freely do I share the good news of His sacrificial love?

How can I be a living sacrifice, to enter into a new lifestyle, in His resurrection power?

Contemplations Response

_____

_____

_____

_____

_____

_____

_____

_____

_____

_____

_____

_____

_____

Lord, what would You desire to say to me today?

_____

_____

_____

_____

_____

_____

_____

_____

_____

_____

_____

_____

ACTIVATION PRAYER

Perfect my heart and life, to stand again, no matter what. Reign and rule in me, King Jesus! Overrule all my flesh. Lord, I release the need to understand more than this— that You know what You are doing, are faithful and true. Enable me, Father God, to spread forth my branches far and wide, that none would be excluded from coming under the great shade of the Tree of LIFE You have planted in me. Hallelujah!

MY "ALONG THE WAY" STORIES

Keep this journal ready to fill in your stories when they happen!

"He who says he abides in Him ought...to WALK JUST AS HE WALKED."
1 John 2:6

POWER OF THE CROSS

My husband has been impressed to remind me that the greatest miracle of all is the power of Jesus' loving sacrifice on the cross to save us all from our sins.

Amen and hallelujah!

Thank you, Lord for Your great mercy, to forgive us of everything!

If you never prayed to be forgiven, *today can be your day!*

Or perhaps you need this guide to help catch others, as you become a *fisher of men.*

I have a simple **prayer of salvation** offered on the next page.

Know that the Lord can use ANY of us to help people receive His gift of salvation. If you want to help someone receive Jesus, you can remember this simplistic approach:

Please (save me) . . . and thank You!

Of course, anyone can use their own words, too.

Picture a child lifting his arms up to his Daddy.

That's the heart the Father is seeking!

SALVATION PRAYER

Lord, thank You for dying on the cross for all my sins.

I confess I am a sinner. I ask You to forgive me for all my sins.

Thank you for coming to earth to take my guilt away.

I receive Your great gift of love and mercy.

Come into my heart now and live, Lord Jesus!

__THANK YOU, LORD,__ for hearing my prayer and saving me!

I also pray now that you will: Heal me, in my body, soul, and spirit.

Holy Spirit, fill me and baptize me with Your holy fire.

Teach me now to follow You.

Come, be Lord of my life.

Thank You for this promise in Romans 10:9,

__"If you declare with your mouth Jesus is Lord,__
__and believe in your heart that God raised him from the dead,__
__you will be saved!"__

"EVERYONE
who calls on the name of the Lord will be saved!"
Romans 10:13

5

KINGDOM COME!

Matthew 28:19-20, Mark 16:15-20

Acts 1:3-11, 2:1-21, 37-43, 9:1-9, 18:9-11, 2 Corinthians 12:9

APPLICATION

Let Him take all the limits off your mind! Believe that He can minister "great and mighty things" in you—*for His Kingdom to come and His will to be done* miraculously through you!

When the Lord unexpectedly impressed me to add these last five chapters, He highlighted these three components to share about this event. The following applications are to establish the "new norm" for advancing His Kingdom.

A. Ascension and Commission

The Lord gave strategic instructions to the disciples just prior to His departure, commissioning them to go global! These words of impartation stretched far beyond the initial commissioning of the Twelve.

The Great Commission: **"All authority in heaven and on earth has been given to me. Therefore, go and make disciples of all nations, baptizing them in the name of the Father and of the Son and of the Holy Spirit, and teaching them to obey everything I have commanded you. And surely, I am with you always, to the very end of the age."** (Matthew 28:19-20 NIV)

Since the Lord gave such incredible mandates and promises just before ascending; their future loomed larger than ever! They would be on their own, missing the physical presence of Jesus, but with a promise of His continued power and protection. His ultimate plan for the ages was finally being released, *to do the extraordinary through the ordinary*, through them and through all of us.

B. Transitioning from Jesus to the Holy Spirit

The Lord had a way of lassoing their old thoughts and ways with brilliant new paradigms. This transition time after His departure, into their new season of ministry without His physical presence, brought them all together seeking His wisdom. They knew they had to do things His way, and fortunately remembered His admonition: **"On one occasion, while He was eating with them, He gave them this command: 'Do not leave Jerusalem, but wait for the gift my Father promised, which you have heard me speak about. For John baptized with water, but in a few days you will be baptized with the Holy Spirit . . . But you will receive power when the Holy Spirit comes on you; and you will be my witnesses in Jerusalem, and in all Judea and Samaria, and to the ends of the earth.'"** (Acts 1:4-5, 8 NIV)

And so, they waited. They likely did not expect the wind or fire, or the noise that blasted them from heaven itself!

"When the day of Pentecost came, they were all together in one place. Suddenly a sound [Greek: blast, sound] **like the blowing of a violent wind came from heaven and filled the whole house where they were sitting. They saw what seemed to be tongues of fire that separated and came to rest on each of them. All of them were filled with the Holy Spirit and began to speak in other tongues as the Spirit enabled them. Now there were staying in Jerusalem God-fearing Jews from every nation under heaven. When they heard this sound, a crowd came together in bewilderment, because each one heard their own language being spoken."** (Acts 2:1-6 NIV) *Fifteen languages are listed in Acts 2:8-11.*

The fear of the Lord came upon them all anew and afresh.
New power began surging forth through Peter:

"In the last days, God says, 'I will pour out my Spirit on all people. Your sons and daughters will prophesy, your young men will see visions, your old men will dream dreams. Even on my servants, both men and women, I will pour out my Spirit in those days, and they will prophesy'. . .And everyone who calls on the name of the Lord will be saved." (Acts 2:17-18, 21 NIV)

The eyes of the crowd now focused fully on Peter.

"Those who accepted his message were baptized, and about 3,000 were added to their number that day! They devoted themselves to the apostles' teaching and to

fellowship, to the breaking of bread and to prayer. Everyone was filled with awe at the many wonders and signs performed by the apostles." (Acts 2:41-43 NIV)

C. Subsequent Workers to Advance the Kingdom

20 Years Later. One moment Saul could be seen charging ahead on his high horse to slaughter followers of Jesus, and the next moment they saw him blindly eating dust, crying out, ***"Who are you LORD?!"*** (See Acts 9:5.)

The Lord blinded him to give him his spiritual eyesight. Suddenly this zealous persecutor became a zealous missionary, by the grace of God. The Lord specializes in calling the least likely candidates for His incredible plan to save and transform the world. Saul/Paul seems to represent all of us who have been delivered from darkness into His powerful Light, who have come to Him after the Lord's physical time upon the earth.

Jesus has a special invitation and plan for all of us. Our expectancy for His work through us should always be seen just as significant as it was for Saul, wherever and whenever we are planted into God's family.

He has entrusted all the work of His kingdom into our hands today in the same three ways:

A. *We too* are commissioned and sent forth to impact the globe.

B. *We too* are empowered by the outpouring of the Holy Spirit for great service.

C. *We too* are blessed and entrusted like Paul, with the Lord's abiding presence and promise to work His great signs through us.

WE ARE His plan upon the earth today. We must know this, receive His impartation of power, and expect to function in His great supernatural power. The Holy Spirit will equip each of us for all these works that we have studied. As we align with His plan, our faith will increase, and His power will be imparted to us to bless our world and to advance His Kingdom.

I must confess that I only slowly began to realize this in my extensive study of His miracles. *We are His plan upon the earth today!* I do not need to plead to be His hands and feet, rather I have already been entrusted and commissioned with this honor, privilege, and responsibility before Jesus ever left the earth.

"For the kingdom of God is not in word but in power." (1 Corinthians 4:20)

"Whoever believes in Me will do the works I have been doing, and they will do even greater things than these, because I am going to the Father. And I will do whatever

you ask in My name, so that the Father may be glorified in the Son."
(John 14:12-13 NIV)

OBSERVATIONS OF THE BIBLICAL ACCOUNT

1. Ascension had only been mentioned once by Jesus to His followers as part of the unfolding plan! They were continually tried and tested to trust His **unpredictable** ways.

2. I have long had the impression that there was a real significance to the actual ascension that I have never heard discussed. I believe that He was demonstrating to us that even in the heavens above, He would be **untouchable** by other spiritual beings.

Biblically, there would be a prophetic fulfillment linked to His ascension, as announced by the "two men dressed in white."

"This same Jesus, who has been taken from you into heaven, will come back in the same way you have seen Him go into heaven." (Acts 1:11)

COMMUNION

Open my heart, Holy Spirit, to be still and listen to Your heart. Help me to receive and believe. Prepare me for powerful new activation.

Biblical Applications and Observations

_____

_____

_____

_____

_____

_____

_____

_____

_____

_____

_____

_____

ALONG THE WAY Reflections (on the author's story)

_____

_____

_____

_____

_____

_____

_____

_____

_____

_____

_____

_____

CONTEMPLATIONS

What hindrances do you see in my heart, Lord?

How do I need to activate my faith to do the "greater works?"

How should I yield more fully to the Holy Spirit to ascend with my Lord in new ways?

Contemplations Response

Lord, what would You desire to say to me today?

ACTIVATION PRAYER

I am saying YES to your Great Commission in my life, O Lord. Use me to do the works that You have done. Prepare me for the greater things. Awaken me to receive revelations in Your Word, by Your Holy Spirit, deep unto deep! May I never settle for the way things have been. Rather, may I be reinvigorated in my spirit to go forth in daily obedience, and see You release Your supernatural life through mine. So be it!

MY "ALONG THE WAY" STORIES

Keep this journal ready to fill in your stories when they happen!

"He who says he abides in Him ought...to WALK JUST AS HE WALKED."
1 John 2:6

PRAYER OF SURRENDER

Your Kingdom come,
Your will be done in me today!

I surrender all.
I lay aside all that hinders
and fully yield to your Holy Spirit.
Not my will, Yours be done.

Fill my heart with Your compassion
to "so love" the world,
that I will give my time, my energy,
and my life for others.

I give you my heart,
My hands, my feet.

I receive Your anointing to go forth in Jesus Name,
to be,
"GOING yet BE PROCLAIMING
saying that the kingdom of heaven has neared,
be CURING the infirmed...
dead ones BE ROUSING!"
Matthew 10:7 Greek Interlinear

So be it!

INDEX
"ALONG THE WAY" STORIES

EPILOGUE

AUTHOR'S NOTE

I am delighted that you have taken this journey with me! As I originally followed Jesus through a study of His miracles, I thought it would be for my own benefit. The Lord surprised me as He led me to share it with the world, and now you have followed my journey.

Let my journey become your journey!

As you have plunged into the ***His Hands, My Feet: Study Journal,*** I trust that the Applications and Observations from my original Bible study have helped to deepen your communion with Christ. I hope the Contemplations helped readjust some old mindsets. If you took the time to ask the Lord to speak, and journaled His reply, that has likely been your deepest joy.

My passion is to see the entire body of Christ GROW in compassion, surrender, and a *daily demonstration of His power being released in each one of us!*

Go for it! KNOW that He wants to do His mighty works through YOU!

If you would like to share a part of your journey from studying these accounts and activating yourself in new ways, I would love to hear your stories and/or some "Along the Way" times with Him! How do you feel better prepared to follow Him?

I say "Amen" to His work in you and through you as *His hands work through YOUR feet!*

Blessings from your sister in the Lord,

Gail Okuley

HisHandsMyFeet@Outlook.com

www.ingramcontent.com/pod-product-compliance
Lightning Source LLC
Chambersburg PA
CBHW041136120626
46547CB00020B/3015